Dedicated to those who write and illustrate their own life stories in scrapbook pages.

Managing Editor MaryJo Regier
Editor Emily Curry Hitchingham
Art Director Nick Nyffeler
Graphic Designers Jordan Kinney, Robin Rozum
Art Acquisitions Editor Janetta Abucejo Wieneke
Craft Editor Jodi Amidei
Photographer Ken Trujillo
Contributing Photographer Lizzy Creazzo, Jennifer Reeves
Contributing Writers Heather A. Eades, Angie Pedersen
Editorial Support Karen Cain, Amy Glander, Dena Twinem
Contributing Memory Makers Masters Jessie Baldwin, Valerie Barton,
Joanna Bolick, Jennifer Bourgeault, Jenn Brookover,, Christine Brown, Susan Cyrus, Lisa Dixon, Sheila Doherty, Kathy Fesmire, Diana Graham,
Angie Head, Jodi Heinen, Jeniece Higgins, Nicola Howard, Julie Johnson, Kelli Noto, Heidi Schueller, Torrey Scott, Trudy Sigurdson, Shannon
Taylor, DeniseTucker, Andrea Lyn Vetten-Marley, Samantha Walker, SharonWhitehead, Holle Wiktorek

Memory Makers® *Your Scrapbook Your Story*

Published by Memory Makers Books, an imprint of F+W Publications, Inc.
12365 Huron Street, Suite 500, Denver, CO 80234
Phone (800) 254-9124
First edition. Printed in the United States.
09 08 07 06 05 5 4 3 2 1

Library of Congress Cataloging-in-Publication Data

Your scrapbook your story / [editor, Emily Curry Hitchingham].
p. cm.
Includes index.
ISBN 1-892127-60-1
1. Photograph albums. 2. Photographs--Conservation and restoration. 3. Scrapbooks. I.
Hitchingham, Emily Curry. II. Memory Makers Books.

TR465.Y68 2005
745.593--dc22

2005049554

Distributed to trade and art markets by
F+W Publications, Inc.
4700 East Galbraith Road, Cincinnati, OH 45236
Phone (800) 289-0963
ISBN 1-892127-60-1

Distributed in Canada by Fraser Direct
100 Armstrong Avenue
Georgetown, ON, Canada L7G 5S4
Tel: (905) 877-4411

Distributed in the U.K. and Europe by David & Charles
Brunel House, Newton Abbot, Devon, TQ12 4PU, England
Tel: (+44) 1626 323200, Fax: (+44) 1626 323319
E-mail: mail@davidandcharles.co.uk

Distributed in Australia by Capricorn Link
P.O. Box 704, S. Windsor NSW, 2756 Australia
Tel: (02) 4577-3555

Memory Makers Books is the home of *Memory Makers*, the scrapbook magazine dedicated to educating and
inspiring scrapbookers. To subscribe, or for more information, call (800) 366-6465.
Visit us on the Internet at www.memorymakersmagazine.com.

Foreword

There's an African proverb that says, "When an old man dies, a library burns." Is your library already smoldering?

When I first started scrapbooking, I could not wait to get started on the boxes of photos I had gathered of my kids over the years. I was so excited to finally have a means of telling the stories of my children's lives. Soon I realized scrapbooking was the perfect hobby for me—creativity with a purpose. After a couple of years, however, I noticed something was missing from my scrapbooks. Me.

While I was working so hard to creatively preserve my family's memories, I often forgot to tell my own stories. I came to realize that if something happened to me, my kids would turn to my scrapbooks for comfort. Yet they wouldn't find me there. When you take all the pictures and aren't in any of them, you become a "silent partner" in your family's history. Would the person viewing your albums know that you were at every soccer game? Would they know you attended every choir performance? Though you may be present to record the events, your personal likeness and perspective is often lost without layouts that capture how you contribute to, not just chronicle, special memories. Otherwise, your voice is silenced and your stories disappear.

Let this book serve as a "light bulb moment" for you; it's important to scrapbook about yourself and it's important that you start now. Consider preserving your piece of the family puzzle your duty to your loved ones. You can help document family history, traditions and cultural heritage by highlighting your part in the process. Future genealogists will thank you for making their job easier by providing the details of your life as they unfold. Moreover, your scrapbooks let you tell your stories the way only you can. And if you don't tell your stories, who will? Do you really want to leave it to your husband or your children to recount your life's memories? Would their recollections best represent who you are? You are the only one with these memories, these friends and these dreams. You are the only YOU you have to share with the people in your life.

In all, you have unique talents, interests and passions. You've lived a life worth remembering. Your stories are worth telling. Let the ideas and projects in this book inspire you to begin. In so doing, your library survives far beyond your years to enlighten and inspire those around you.

Angie

Angie Pedersen

Angie Pedersen is a professional scrapbooking instructor and author of *The Book of Me, Growing Up Me* and *The Book of Us*. You can visit her online at www.OneScrappySite.com.

Table of Contents

I am...

Pages that pin down personal characteristics, qualities, little-known facts, favorites, life roles and more

I feel...

Pages that explore emotional reveries on aging, change, challenges, contentment, thankfulness, perseverance and more

I believe...

Pages that embody personal faith, philosophy, spirituality, principles, insights and more

I know...

Pages that profess strongly held personal truths, convictions, life lessons, words of wisdom, reflections and more

I aspire...

Pages that reveal ambitions, aspirations, resolutions, goals, new beginnings and more

Note to Self: p. 67

I cherish...

Pages that feature greatest loves, special treasures, beloved pastimes, favorite indulgences and more

Note to Self: p. 78

I achieve...

Pages that celebrate emotional, physical and professional accomplishments

Note to Self: p. 91

I contribute...

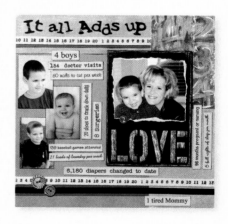

Pages that recognize contributions to family and vocation

Note to Self: p. 102

TABLE OF CONTENTS 5

Introduction

Scrapbooking is all about stories. From the birth of brand-new life to reflective tribute pages, documenting our memories is first and foremost a means of keeping a legacy alive. Long before our hands ever assemble and adorn a scrapbook page exist the emotions, personalities and experiences that first touched our hearts. These memories strung together create a synopsis of our lives, complete with chapters, characters, settings and story lines. Our scrapbooks, in turn, are storybooks we author.

Oftentimes, however, we focus so intently upon narrating the stories of others that we forget the importance of sharing our own. We overlook that we are protagonists in our own life adventures, whose stories are part of a shared family anthology. Because our lives are interconnected with those of our loved ones, this combined history will be incomplete if we are absent from its pages. As scrapbookers, we have recognized the value of preserving and passing along those chronicles closest to our hearts. It is important that we turn a new page and mark our own place in time with no less dedication.

Your Scrapbook Your Story was generated to encourage you to do just that: design your own pages in time, from your perspective and by your hands. Expressing yourself in the form of art, photography and journaling is a wonderful opportunity to both share slices of your life and exercise your creativity. You'll be surprised by how enjoyable and emotionally rewarding the process can be—and by how much of yourself there is to share that you may have undervalued in the past. In surveying the pages featured, you'll find any reasons you've had for postponing scrapbooking about yourself will be replaced with inspiration to begin. Chapters devoted to exploring a different component of your one-of-a-kind personality ensure that no aspect of yourself or your story will be missed, including your characteristics, emotions, thoughts, convictions, beliefs, greatest loves, ambitions and achievements. Moreover, each wonderful piece of artwork is as unique as the artist who created it, spanning a spectrum of styles from insightful and introspective to fun and lighthearted. We've also included examples of endearing mini self-themed albums, as well as thought-provoking sidebars sure to spur your imagination.

If you're holding this book, you've made the decision to ensure the presence of your personality, experiences and perspective in your scrapbooks—and more important, in the stories that will be handed down over time. Every photo and journaling entry will be like a fingerprint or signature—attributed only to you, artfully and unmistakably acknowledging you were here. So enjoy the process. Explore, express and rediscover yourself in your pages. Then share your story in progress with your own eager and captive audience.

Emily

Emily Curry Hitchingham, Associate Editor

Ideas for all-about-me mini albums

Small-size and alternative-format albums are a fun approach and easy-to-accomplish alternative to full-size self pages and albums. These minimized masterpieces boast dimensional, interactive and tactile qualities that will make it hard for admirers to resist exploring them—all the while learning more about the artists behind their creation.

Favorites Tag Book

The thought of creating 12 x 12" pages somewhat overwhelmed Alecia, but she nonetheless wanted to create an All-About-Me album. This tag book was the perfect way to start recording her thoughts and memories in a small-scale, unique and altogether whimsical way. Each embellished cardstock tag reflects on the major priorities in her life, as well as passions, wishes and fond memories. Alecia linked the tags on one large binder ring, making this project the perfect catalyst for beginning a larger album about herself, within which she can include this tag book in a page pocket.

Alecia Ackerman Grimm, Atlanta, Georgia

Tidbits About Me

Paper bags proved to be the perfect supply for Melissa to create a fun and resourceful mini book about herself. Journaling tags with colorful ribbon toppers are tucked inside each cropped paper bag "page," taking the viewer on a whirlwind tour of Melissa's world with each category. Lively colors, textures and shapes dance about each page, offset by the earthy brown of the paper bags. It was this punchy little project that ultimately inspired Melissa to begin an 8 x 8" album as well.

Melissa Godin, Lorne, New Brunswick, Canada

Colleen

An ordinary resource can make extraordinary art, as Colleen demonstrates in this 16-page mini album. She created this unique assemblage from paper lunch bags that she wet, crumpled, ironed, then stained with walnut ink and color wash. Each page illustrates a different role and description of her character through photos and tactile décor. She bound the book with twine and used black-and-white images for a cohesive feel. Tucked into the lunch bag openings, Colleen conceals her deepest loves, fears, feelings and dreams.

Colleen Stearns,
Natrona Heights, Pennsylvania

Thankful Box and Blessing Booklet

Celebrating 20 years of marriage and seven years as a cancer survivor, Cheryl created this box and accordion booklet as a gift to her family to represent the many blessings in her life. She chose to feature her four most precious life roles: wife, mother, friend and scrapbooker. Both box and book were designed with an autumn theme—the season to remember to always give thanks. Each page of Cheryl's booklet contains a pocketed pullout tag adorned with photos and season-inspired accents. The paper and paint-altered wooden box boasts stitching, a stencil tag accent and leaves given a "dewy" effect with clear embossing powder and a clear watermark pen.

Cheryl Mezzetti,
Weymouth, Massachusetts

Finding Me Again

Colleen created this booklet to disclose her recent struggles with a downtrodden spirit. Much like her feelings, it is worn and slightly distressed, but touched with distinct elements of cheer and beauty embodied in pretty ribbons, soft flowers, delicate lace accents, as well as photos bearing the encouraging smiles of her husband and children—the support system that is seeing her through. Aged tags contain Colleen's journaling, and a mini accordion element containing a favorite quote can be found beneath the flower on the booklet's cover.

*Colleen Stearns,
Natrona Heights, Pennsylvania*

I am...

the sum of my little-known factoids and favorite things. An assortment of unique qualities, characteristics and quirks. A combination of complicated and simple, straightforward and sideways, silly and sophisticated, even keel and off kilter. I am the totality of my traits. The culmination of my nuances and idiosyncrasies. I am distinctive. Entirely original. Without duplication. I am the one and only me.

THIS

Did you know thi... me!

I love to listen to Angel sing. I could listen to her...

At McDonalds I always order #2 with no pickles and...

PHOTOGRAPHER

MY FAVORITE COLOR IS RE...

MOM TO THREE

I love chocolate!! I could eat it anytime of the day or night!

I love listening to Disco and 80's music

I'm a huge Survivor fan! I've watched every season!

My favorite foods are steak, hamburgers, and Chinese food.

SCRAPPER

I can't stand to cook! I do like to bake.

I love this picture! It shows the happy person that I am, and that is what I want everyone to know about me! I'm always happy! I love my late night chats with Angel. The smile that Jeremy gets when he sees me, and my little Sierras beautiful face! I feel so lucky to have a beautiful family.
...s me at 33! This has been a...

imagine

Virgo

Finding her personality to be true to her astrological sign, Ann-Marie designed her page around the characteristics of a Virgo. She downloaded her descriptions from an astrology Web site, then printed them onto a transparency, highlighting several of the traits she wanted to emphasize. She kept her composition true to her sign by using clean lines and a simple, organized structure.

Ann-Marie Weis, Oakland, California
Photo: Suzy West, Fremont, California

Supplies: Patterned papers, metal frame, square brads (Chatterbox); textured cardstock (Bazzill); square frame (Scrapworks); vintage flash card; ribbons; transparency

Top-10 Things You Don't Know About Me

Jessie designed her own top-10 list to reveal personalized trivia about herself. From secret crushes to favorite morning rituals, each fact box shares a piece of Jessie's life that makes her who she is today. Warm, bright colors give her page a sunny feel to reflect her smiling disposition in the photos. To dress up the metal stencil letters in the center of the photos, Jessie first sanded them with fine-grained sandpaper, then painted them with two coats of paint, lightly inking the edges once dry.

Jessie Baldwin, Las Vegas, Nevada

Supplies: Patterned paper (Magenta); textured cardstock (Bazzill); letter and number stamps (Hero Arts, Ma Vinci's Reliquary); rectangle stamp (Postmodern Design); metal stencil letters (Colorbök); stamping ink; acrylic paints; pen

Simply *Sam*

The colors red and black, an old brooch, festive strings—these are a few of Sam's favorite things. Samantha designed her page to reflect the eccentric and dynamic aspects of her personality, utilizing layers of textures and bold colors to express her qualities and passions. She included a mini book, pocketed on the left and held fast by her favorite brooch, which lays out the loves of her life. To add a variegated edge to her focal-point photo, Samantha simply printed the image onto photo paper and used a paintbrush and water to bleed the inks.

Samantha Walker, Battle Ground, Washington

Supplies: Patterned paper, textured paper, velvet paper and mesh paper (FLAX art & design); letter stamp, watermark ink (Stampin' Up!); sheer black fabric (Carole Fabrics); photo corners (Boutique Trims); liquid gold pen (Marvy); red and black cord; eyelets; embossing powder; cardstock; vellum

Me

Lisa took a glimpse at her life and identity at age 38 and celebrated with a carefree layout. She listed her trademark hobbies and habits on stapled strips of paper embellished with ribbon tabs. Plastic slide holders filled with mini collaged accents play up the "staples" of her life, which include Krispy Kremes, MTV, being a wife and mom—symbols that bring fact and fun together.

Lisa Cole, Puyallup, Washington

Supplies: Patterned papers, epoxy sticker, letter stickers (Creative Imaginations); decorative metal frame (JewelCraft); wooden letters, decorative rub-on, bottle cap, canvas letters (Li'l Davis Designs); stick pin, paper clip (EK Success); foam corner stamp, metal-rimmed circle tag, staples, safety pin, metal flower brad, rub-on letters (Making Memories); shaped brads (Chatterbox); die cuts, number stickers (KI Memories); twist tie, sticker tag (Pebbles); metal label holders (source unknown); plastic slide holders; acrylic paint; ribbons

Eight Random Facts About Me

Kim wanted to create a layout about things people may not know about her and decided to go digital to do so. Her self-portrait was taken with a digital photo set on a timer, and the page elements, including monogram letter stickers, were created through the use of image-editing software.

Kim Mauch, Portland, Oregon

Supplies: Image-editing software (Adobe Photoshop Elements); Tanya Todd-Krason papers (www.playonelements.com)

CHERISH (cher´·ish) 1. to hold dear 2. to treasure, adore, value, and love

MOTHER WIFE FRIEND

Valerie

ENDURING (en·door´·ing) 1. lasting; permanent 2. continuing on until the end

Valerie

Family defines what is most important to Valerie, and she designed this heart-warming layout to express that fact. She used the above page for her self-portrait, utilizing file tabs to list the roles she plays as mother, wife and friend in her family. For the second page, she created a gridlike assemblage of black-and-white family photos enhanced with artful text to express her bond with each family member. Valerie kept her layout simple with a classic feel, yet included stitching, buttons and ribbon accents for homespun charm.

Valerie Salmon, Carmel, Indiana

Supplies: Patterned papers (Karen Foster Design, Paper Company); textured cardstock (Bazzill); rub-on letters (Making Memories); acrylic buttons, metal buttons (K & Company); letter beads (Westrim); letter stickers (EK Success); metal-rimmed tag (Avery); ribbon (Offray); label maker (Dymo); safety pin; string; sewing machine

FOREVER (for·ev´·er) 1. for always, without end 2. without the bonds of time; eternal

SALMON

family

The heart's treasure is life's truest wealth.

About Me in 2003

Being the list-maker that she is, Vicki put her skills to good use to define how she thought of herself in 2003. She created tags to describe who she was, where she went, what she did and what she loved during that year and then stitched each tag into place. Shimmering blue ribbon brings sophisticated shine to her soft design, while large number stamps bearing the year cleverly contain her name within one of the zeros for a subtle, playful touch.

Vicki Harvey, Champlin, Minnesota

Supplies: Patterned paper (Mustard Moon); textured cardstock (Bazzill); photo corners (Canson); ribbon, ribbon slides, metal-rimmed circle tag (Making Memories); epoxy letters (Li'l Davis Designs); small letter stamps (Bunch Of Fun); large number stamps (Ma Vinci's Reliquary); stamping ink

Pieces of Me

The many pieces of Jeniece come together on this layout, paying tribute to the many treasured roles in her life. Using image-editing software, Jeniece altered her self-portrait to have a puzzlelike effect, which coordinates with the actual personalized puzzle beside it. Rub-ons, stamps and her own handwriting are featured on individual puzzle pieces to represent each role she embraces. Jeniece included a mini book at the bottom of the page, which includes photographs and provides additional details.

Jeniece Higgins, Lake Forest, Illinois

Supplies: Patterned papers (Basic Grey, Rusty Pickle); mailbox letters, foam letter stamps, mini album, rub-on words (Making Memories); stamps (Hero Arts, Ma Vinci's Reliquary, PSX Design); ribbon (Rusty Pickle); rub-on words (Provo Craft); image-editing software (Adobe Photoshop Elements); solvent ink (Tsukineko); acrylic paint; blank puzzle

A Little Flawed, A *Little* Flawless

In this self-discovery spread, Samuel listed both the ticks and terrific talents that make up the whole of who he is. For the qualities he listed on his "Flawed" side of the spread, he cut out pieces of the photos and replaced them with journaling strips arranged in a disorderly fashion. Samuel kept the qualities he enjoys about himself well-organized on the "Flawless" page, using a square punch to showcase physical attributes he favors.

Samuel Cole, Stillwater, Minnesota

Supplies: Patterned paper (Chatterbox); textured cardstock (Bazzill); square punches (EK Success, Creative Memories); circle punch (Punch Bunch); rub-on letters (Li'l Davis Designs, Making Memories); cardstock; pen

Note to self

Creating pages about ourselves requires accepting that doing so is hardly selfish; rather, it is selfless. Simply said, we need to "get over ourselves." It's hard for many people to create self-centered pages because they struggle with their self-concepts. They complain that they don't like photos of themselves because they aren't at their ideal weight, they're unhappy with their haircut or they are not wearing makeup. Consequently they refuse to allow family members to take their picture. Here's a news flash—even if there are no pictures of you, people still know what you look like. You're not keeping it a secret. The people in your life are aware of your appearance when you're sick, when you're in your sweats and when you first get up in the morning—and love you regardless. It's crucial to put aside whatever value judgment you place on yourself and your stories and scrapbook them anyway. Once you move past your personal hang-ups and insecurities, you give the people in your life the gift of yourself. Better yet, you may even begin to see in yourself the wonderful things they see.

My Life By the Numbers

Missy's photoless layout reveals the digits that document her life thus far. Underneath each number sticker-adorned square lies the meaning behind each, including the number of times Missy has moved, the depth of her deepest scuba dive and her highest bowling score, to list just a few. To arrange her interactive elements, Missy alternated between scoring and mounting the paper squares directly to the page with eyelets or attaching them to lengths of ribbon.

Missy Partridge, Whaleyville, Maryland

Supplies: Patterned papers (Basic Grey, Rusty Pickle); leather flowers, metal flowers, fabric flowers, metal numbers (Making Memories); label maker (Dymo); number stickers, label sticker, letter stickers (Creative Imaginations); eyelets; stamping ink; rickrack; various ribbons

If I Am Not I

Miki has always been the photographer in her family, so her scrapbooks have always been about everybody else. However, now that her husband is hooked on digital photography, there are lots of great photos of Miki to include on pages about herself. She included a journaling book on this, her first self-layout, to add more photos and have space to share her hopes, dreams, loves and loathes, as well as to express who she is and what she does. Miki printed her journaling on transparencies for a glossy shine that keeps her page sophisticated and formal.

Miki Benedict, Modesto, California
Photo: Keith Benedict, Modesto, California

Supplies: Patterned papers, tags, labels (Basic Grey); vellum quote (Memories Complete); chipboard letter (Making Memories); button (Doodlebug Design); family stamp (Hero Arts); ribbons (7 Gypsies); solvent ink (Tsukineko); acrylic paint; transparencies; assorted ribbons and fibers; silk flower

Who I Am

Scrapbooking has become such an integral part of who Patti is that she had to create a space for it on this layout dedicated to her many roles. She staggered her journaling on overlapping tags that define her identity to her family, friends and self. Wooden art chips and labels were used for a timeless feel and a label-maker label beside the image of her family to illustrate her treasured new "name."

Patti Milazzo, Lexington, South Carolina

Supplies: Patterned papers (Li'l Davis Designs); textured cardstock (Bazzill); letter stamps (PSX Design, Stamp Craft); wood art chip, wood "family" label (Go West Studios); ribbon (May Arts); skeleton leaf (Graphic Products Corp.); mini brads, decorative brads (Making Memories); label maker (Dymo); watermark ink, solvent ink (Tsukineko); staples; acrylic paint

Me

On this page, warm, rich colors, subtle textures and cheerful patterns all help to portray Tracy's personality, which is also exemplified with several carefully chosen defining words. The inviting color scheme conveys a friendly overtone while allowing the eyes to embrace the black-and-white photo. Using clear ink to stamp her name along the left side of the page lends a hint of playfulness and carries visual interest across the page.

Tracy Kuethe, Milford, Ohio
Photo: Beverly Anderson, Cincinnati, Ohio

Supplies: Patterned papers (Chatterbox); textured cardstock (Bazzill); number stickers (Bo-Bunny Press); word stickers (Mrs. Grossman's); ribbon (Offray); foam letter stamps, date stamp (Making Memories); heart stamp (Stampin' Up!); letter stamps (Hero Arts); watermark ink (Ranger); eyelets; fabric; stamping ink; acrylic paint

The ABCs of *Me*

Using the alphabet as her guide, Janelle created a descriptive-word list of her many qualities, using one trait per letter. She kept her layout simple and sweet, using feminine colors and patterns to complement her personality and to coordinate with the tones of the black-and-white self-portrait. Label-maker labels and large title stamps bring a bold touch to the soft design.

Janelle Richmond, Friendswood, Texas

Supplies: Patterned paper (Chatterbox); textured cardstocks (Bazzill); letter stamps (Hero Arts, PSX Design, Stamp Craft); photo turns, brads, foam letter stamps, rub-on numbers (Making Memories); label maker (Dymo); cardstock; acrylic paint; stamping ink

My Top-10 *Secrets*

Stephanie listed her top-10 components of living a joyful life, but also included a journaling passage to detail how at times she struggles to follow her own advice. Stephanie's faith-based tenants are showcased on torn and inked cardstock and a black-and-white photo showcases a sincere smile. Festive colors and frazzled fibers create a sense of playfulness and authenticity.

Stephanie Allbaugh, Appleton, Wisconsin Photo: Carol McCracken, Hamilton, Michigan

Supplies: Patterned paper (Karen Foster Design); textured cardstock (Bazzill); letter tile stickers, mini brads (Making Memories); letter stickers (Me & My Big Ideas); letter stamps (Ma Vinci's Reliquary); fibers (Bazzill, Fiber Scraps); label maker (Dymo); solvent ink (Tsukineko); paint; stamping ink; spiral clip; silk flowers

A Part of Me

Listing the traits she inherited from each parent's nationality, Teresa used this page as a celebration of her unique heritage and characteristics. She created a column for both the Japanese and Caucasian physical traits she exhibits, placing them directly above her self-portrait. Teresa was born in the year of the Dragon and handcut the Kanji symbol for "dragon" from cardstock to add visual energy.

Teresa Olier, Colorado Springs, Colorado

Supplies: Textured cardstocks (Bazzill); metal word charm (KI Memories)

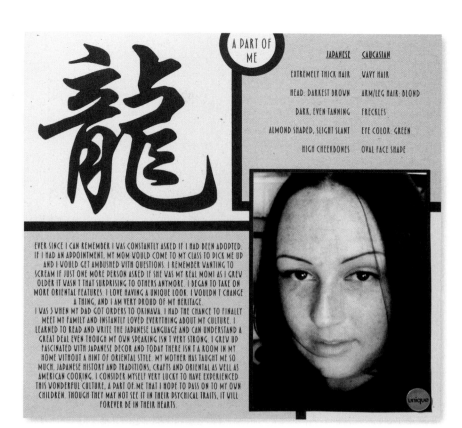

A PART OF ME

JAPANESE	CAUCASIAN
EXTREMELY THICK HAIR	WAVY HAIR
HEAD: DARKEST BROWN	ARM/LEG HAIR: BLOND
DARK, EVEN TANNING	FRECKLES
ALMOND SHAPED, SLIGHT SLANT	EYE COLOR: GREEN
HIGH CHEEKBONES	OVAL FACE SHAPE

EVER SINCE I CAN REMEMBER I WAS CONSTANTLY ASKED IF I HAD BEEN ADOPTED. IF I HAD AN APPOINTMENT, MY MOM WOULD COME TO MY CLASS TO PICK ME UP AND I WOULD GET AMBUSHED WITH QUESTIONS. I REMEMBER WANTING TO SCREAM IF JUST ONE MORE PERSON ASKED IF SHE WAS MY REAL MOM! AS I GREW OLDER IT WASN'T THAT SURPRISING TO OTHERS ANYMORE. I BEGAN TO TAKE ON MORE ORIENTAL FEATURES. I LOVE HAVING A UNIQUE LOOK. I WOULDN'T CHANGE A THING, AND I AM VERY PROUD OF MY HERITAGE. I WAS 5 WHEN MY DAD GOT ORDERS TO OKINAWA. I HAD THE CHANCE TO FINALLY MEET MY FAMILY AND INSTANTLY LOVED EVERYTHING ABOUT MY CULTURE. I LEARNED TO READ AND WRITE THE JAPANESE LANGUAGE AND CAN UNDERSTAND A GREAT DEAL EVEN THOUGH MY OWN SPEAKING ISN'T VERY STRONG. I GREW UP FASCINATED WITH JAPANESE DECOR AND TODAY THERE ISN'T A ROOM IN MY HOME WITHOUT A HINT OF ORIENTAL STYLE. MY MOTHER HAS TAUGHT ME SO MUCH. JAPANESE HISTORY AND TRADITIONS, CRAFTS AND ORIENTAL AS WELL AS AMERICAN COOKING. I CONSIDER MYSELF VERY LUCKY TO HAVE EXPERIENCED THIS WONDERFUL CULTURE, A PART OF ME THAT I HOPE TO PASS ON TO MY OWN CHILDREN. THOUGH THEY MAY NOT SEE IT IN THEIR PHYSICAL TRAITS, IT WILL FOREVER BE IN THEIR HEARTS.

This is **me**. It is Monday morning and I am supposed to be vacuuming.

I am 42 years young.

I am a mother, a wife, a sister and a daughter.

My favorite color is green!

I have red hair that I inherited from my grandfather.

I hate being late.

I am not a very good housekeeper. I am a good cook.

I wish I would laugh more and be a bit sillier.

I love antiques and things that are handmade.

I need to lose 10 pounds.

I have a beautiful, smart, vibrant daughter. She brings me joy every day.

My husband is my best friend. I love him completely.

Today, I am comfortable being **me**.

FEB 0 9 2004

This Is Me

LeAnne's layout takes an up-close and personal look at the woman she is inside. Introspective journaling that lists facts, favorites, hopes and dreams creates a reflective tone for her page to accompany her self-portrait. LeAnne printed her photo on canvas, then sanded and inked it for a well-loved look. The ribbon accent in the lower right gives balance and boldness to the page, along with a sense of familiarity and comfort, which is carried throughout the page.

LeAnne B. Fritts, Denver, North Carolina

Supplies: Patterned papers (Anna Griffin); ribbon (Offray); metal box frame (source unknown); photo corners (Canson); pins, eyelets, photo turns (Making Memories); epoxy letter stickers (Creative Imaginations); letter stamps (Stampers Anonymous); date stamp, photo canvas (Office Depot); postage stamp letters (handmade); cardstock; stamping ink; sandpaper

I feel...

peaceful contentment in quiet reprieve. Blissful elation in moments of sheer joy. Thankful for my blessings, challenged by my struggles, humbled by my shortcomings and proud of my strengths. I feel my wisdom growing with the coming of age. My confidence emerging from the hollows of unhappiness. I feel trust in my intuition. Bravery in the face of change. I feel satisfaction in who I have been and who I am becoming.

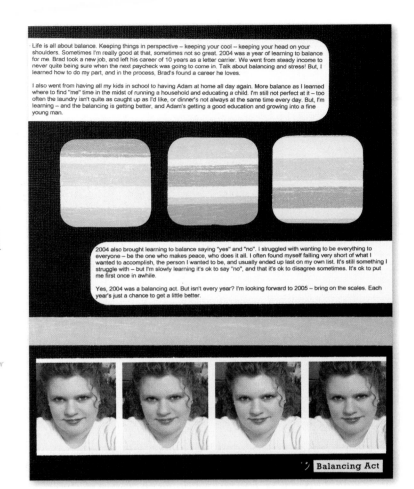

Life is all about balance. Keeping things in perspective – keeping your cool – keeping your head on your shoulders. Sometimes I'm really good at that, sometimes not so great. 2004 was a year of learning to balance for me. Brad took a new job, and left his career of 10 years as a letter carrier. We went from steady income to never quite being sure when the next paycheck was going to come in. Talk about balancing and stress! But, I learned how to do my part, and in the process, Brad's found a career he loves.

I also went from having all my kids in school to having Adam at home all day again. More balance as I learned where to find "me" time in the midst of running a household and educating a child. I'm still not perfect at it – too often the laundry isn't quite as caught up as I'd like, or dinner's not always at the same time every day. But, I'm learning – and the balancing is getting better, and Adam's getting a good education and growing into a fine young man.

2004 also brought learning to balance saying "yes" and "no". I struggled with wanting to be everything to everyone – be the one who makes peace, who does it all. I often found myself falling very short of what I wanted to accomplish, the person I wanted to be, and usually ended up last on my own list. It's still something I struggle with – but I'm slowly learning it's ok to say "no", and that it's ok to disagree sometimes. It's ok to put me first once in awhile.

Yes, 2004 was a balancing act. But isn't every year? I'm looking forward to 2005 – bring on the scales. Each year's just a chance to get a little better.

Balancing Act

Balancing Act

Becky's well-balanced page design embodies the balancing act she perpetually performs in her life. Her husband's career change, the home schooling of her child and the setting of boundaries are all new changes for her to work into the flow of her life. Becky desaturated and tinted her self-portrait using image-editing software, then printed it onto cardstock in a series for an artful illustration of her numerous and varying roles.

Becky Thompson, Fruitland, Idaho

Supplies: Patterned paper (Rusty Pickle); textured cardstock (Bazzill); stickers, heart brad (Making Memories); image-editing software (Adobe Photoshop); corner rounder (Creative Memories); square punch (Marvy)

How can one be in a room crowded and bustling with people and feel completely alone? I am not sure about the science or the sensibility in it, but it happens to me quite frequently. I like to observe what everyone else is doing rather than participating. However, that can get quite lonely. For as long as I can remember, I have always felt this deep sense of loneliness. Maybe it was being a child of divorce or maybe it was always feeling like the odd man out. Yet, I never imagined feeling alone once I was married and started having children. Funny how life works though. During a rough spot early in our marriage, I often felt an overwhelming sense of solitude and isolation in my own home. I remember endless nights of lying in my bed, while Andy was in the next room, feeling such sadness. I was married to a man I loved and adored; yet, there was a chasm between us that seemed unbridgeable. I am glad that he took the first step to start the healing. The sense of loneliness started to disappear. I was so relieved to be able to enjoy coming home each day, instead of dreading what explosion I would face. I am glad that my home is no longer my enemy. However, there are still times when I feel a deep sense of solitude when with a lot of people. Nonetheless, it feels nice to escape from the crowded room sometimes into my own world of thought and imagination. I fear that sometimes my silence and withdrawn nature leads people to assume that I am not a nice person, which couldn't be farther from the truth. I just don't do very well with meeting new people. I enjoy the comfort of old friends and close family. I think that I use my solitude as an escape from putting myself out there, so that I can protect my feelings and prevent hurt. So, I will go on enjoying my solitude, I just hope and pray that the solitude doesn't eat me alive or cost me precious friendships which never had a chance to emerge.

Journaling: November 7, 2004

S·T·Y·L·E

Solitude

Scrapbook pages are often therapeutic, helping to express what often is not completely understood. Feelings of solitude, even when surrounded by people, have long been a part of Christie's soul. She decided to document those feelings on this scrapbook page to better understand them herself and to help her family know more about this hidden part of who she is. She used dark grays and blacks to capture the emotion of loneliness and its resulting imprisonment through the stripes on the ribbons.

Christie Wildes, Gainesville, Florida

Supplies: Patterned paper (Autumn Leaves); textured cardstock (Bazzill); ribbon (Offray); eyelet charm tag, foam letter stamps (Making Memories); acrylic paint; staples

Change Is Good

The look on Elizabeth's face speaks volumes about how a great new haircut can boost one's spirits. After growing her hair out for a lengthy period of time, Elizabeth knew it was time for a change. The bright colors and energetic patterns express the joyful rush that comes with a happy self-image. Journaling tags tucked into a torn pocket further express other people's reactions to Elizabeth's new "do" as well as where she got her inspiration for the look.

Elizabeth Cuzzacrea, Lockport, New York

Supplies: Patterned paper (KI Memories); textured cardstock (Bazzill); letter stickers (Doodlebug Design, Pebbles); rub-on letters (Autumn Leaves); chipboard tiles (Li'l Davis Designs); tags (DMD); ribbons (May Arts); distress ink (Ranger); library pocket; pen; corner rounder

Risk

Erika shares her love for learning and romance on this page dedicated to the risks she feels are worth pursuing in life. By layering and staggering her photos on the upper portion of the page, she provides visual dynamism against her patterned background. A transparent quote sticker placed over cut patterned paper in the lower left corner grounds the page and balances out the journaling block.

Erika Follansbee, Goffstown, New Hampshire
Photos: David Follansbee, Goffstown, New Hampshire

Supplies: Patterned paper (Cross My Heart); quote sticker (Wordsworth)

Simple Dream

Shelley designed this encouraging page to document her struggles with Crohn's disease and to focus on her determination to regain her health. She documented reflections on her journey thus far inside an envelope mounted horizontally across her layout. Shelley repeated the image of herself using a filter on the larger photo. After hearing the Johnny Nash song "I Can See Clearly Now," she took the lyrics to heart and included an excerpt on her page. She transposed the text from the lyrics on one photo using image-editing software to mimic the reflection in the water.

Shelley Rankin,
Fredericton, New Brunswick, Canada

Supplies: Textured cardstock (Bazzill); stickers (Pebbles); ribbons (Making Memories); word pebbles (K & Company); rub-on words (Autumn Leaves, Making Memories); decorative clips (American Traditional Designs, EK Success, 7 Gypsies); metal label holder (Li'l Davis Designs); compass accent (Me & My Big Ideas); letter stencil (Staples); hinge (from local hardware store); image-editing software (Adobe Photoshop); gel pen; large envelope

Self-Discovery

Journaling is very important to Michelle, so one day she decided take photos while logging an entry. The photos included her surroundings and even the journal she was writing in. She manipulated a self-portrait to focus on her eyes and to reflect her mood. Script-style background paper and butterfly accents and stamps were perfect for embodying Michelle's love of journaling and the sense of freedom and change that results from self-discovery.

Michelle Jacknicke, St. Albert, Alberta, Canada

Supplies: Patterned paper (Provo Craft), textured cardstock (Bazzill); printed vellum (Triplets); word stickers (Bo-Bunny Press); letter stickers (EK Success); letter stamps (Making Memories, PSX Design); ribbon (Michaels); slide mounts (DMD); butterfly postage stamps (from Internet); silk butterfly (source unknown); acrylic paint; buttons

Just Do Your Best

Erika proclaims her motto to "Just do your best" on this layout that expresses her acceptance of her strengths and weaknesses. She chose patterned papers with a distressed yet comfortable feel that mesh perfectly with her photo and journaling. Her page comes to terms with the fact that no one is perfect and stresses how important it is to focus on what you are good at rather than what you are not, and to learn something new every day.

Erika Follansbee, Goffstown, New Hampshire
Photo: David Follansbee, Goffstown, New Hampshire

Supplies: Patterned papers (Carolee's Creations, Me & My Big Ideas, Paper Loft); sticker (Karen Foster Design); ribbon sticker (Pebbles); buttons (Making Memories)

As my life progresses, I am becoming acutely aware of what I am good at and what I am not. Its pretty obvious. Some of these things were evident back in school. I was an incredibly good student in all subjects except math. Im still no good at math. My parents just told me to do my best.

Im good at gardening, taking photos (although Im constantly working on getting better), organization, being punctual, researching, and I have a good memory.

Just do your best

Things I am terrible at include: correspondence with friends and family, putting things off until later, eating healthy, thinking on my feet, and keeping up with the news.

I guess it really is important to just do your best, dont beat yourself up for your weaknesses, focus on your strengths, and remember to learn something new every day.

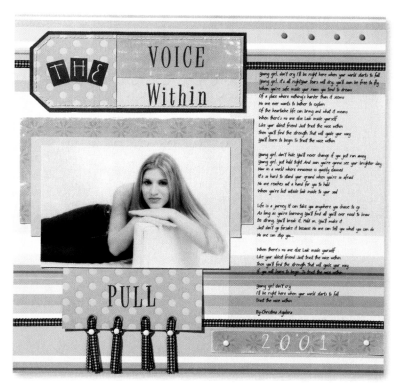

The Voice Within

Courage and strength provided a solid foundation for Nikki's page, which shares her triumph over struggles with an eating disorder and depression. She printed the lyrics of Christina Aguilera's "The Voice Within" on a transparency—a song that has become her personal anthem for its uplifting message of inner strength. Nikki created a journaling card embellished with ribbons that pulls down from underneath her sepia-printed photo.

Nikki Hobbs, Nampa, Idaho
Photo: Artista Photo Lab, San Jose, California

Supplies: Patterned papers (SEI); rub-on letters and numbers (Making Memories); stamps (MoBe' Stamps!); brads; ribbon

To Be Me

Adine wanted to put her thoughts and feelings into her own words on a layout that would serve as a legacy. The left page is distinguished with minimal text and a black-and-white photo on cropped cardstock. The bulk of the right-hand page is comprised of Adine's beliefs, fears and motivations in a free-flowing format on cropped rust-colored cardstock along with a color photo of her face printed on textured paper. By mounting the cardstock elements to paper with printed borders, Adine added an artful look and further enhanced her composition with stamping.

Adine Moynihan, Manchester, Connecticut

Supplies: Patterned paper, stickers (SEI); printed transparency (K & Company); letter stamps (Hero Arts); timepiece stamp (Club Scrap); photo turn, brad (Making Memories); extra thick embossing powder (Suze Weinburg); solvent ink (Tsukineko)

Note to self

Hidden journaling techniques are perfect for housing personal thoughts on your layouts. Here are some ideas to try:

• Pockets: Slip journaling sheets and cards behind matted photos or in pockets made with paper or fabric. Embellish for a decorative touch or adhere to the back of your layout to keep them out of sight. You can note the pocket on the front of your layout ("see back for the full story") or leave it to be discovered later.

• Envelopes: Stationery's answer to hidden journaling. Choose from an array of attractive premade envelopes or fold and decorate your own. Be sure to leave the envelope unsealed so the journaling is easily accessible.

• Cards: Simply fold a piece of cardstock in half and journal on the inside. Mount to the page, add photos or embellishments and, if desired, secure with an attractive closure.

• Mini albums: Add small compact albums you assemble yourself or purchased premade versions you can personalize.

• To make hidden journaling accessible inside a page protector, use a craft knife to cut a slice in the protector over the interactive element. You can also place the piece near the opening of the page protector so the viewer can slip a hand in to reach the journaling with ease.

Me

April was 27 weeks pregnant when this portrait was taken. In realizing over a year later that it was still the most recent photo of her just by herself, she decided to do this page to remember that as much as she loves motherhood, there is more to her identity. Her concealed journaling reflects on how rewarding it is to be so focused on and consumed by the wants and needs of her child, but that it's now time to start remembering who she is as an individual. . .and get another photo of herself taken! April used a ribbon to secure her journaling inside a decorative card, threading the ribbon through the snap in one of the flower accents to secure it closed.

April Peterson, Sacramento, California
Photo: Steve Peterson, Sacramento, California

Supplies: Patterned papers (Chatterbox); textured cardstocks (Bazzill, Chatterbox); ribbon (May Arts); rub-on letters, snaps (Making Memories); flower punch (source unknown); stamping ink

I am 27 weeks pregnant in this photo. This picture is almost a year old, yet it is the most recent photo of me where the focus is 'just me'- not somehow related to the baby.

Looking at this picture, I think about how my life has changed since it was taken.

Xander has taken over my life- but I say this happily. Even as I set out to do a page all about me, his influence finds away in. He's become my life, and for the most part it is wonderful.

I am a mother. I have a son, and I am the world to him. He is a beautiful and delightful boy, and my life feels a little more complete now that he is in it.

Yet... (and how horrible do I feel just typing that three-letter word?) and yet sometimes I feel lost in world that is 'motherhood.' In the beginning it was great to be consumed with his wants and needs and affections- in doing so, I didn't have to think about myself. It was a nice break to not have to dwell on my own.

It was a break, a vacation from myself, but it's time to start coming back. Time to start remembering that I am more than a mother.

Time to get another picture of me taken.

Reality Check

The turbulent, "vandalized" look and feel of Leah's distressed page reflects the personal turmoil she experienced in encountering random acts of violence as a Canadian living in America. Leah and her husband found themselves targets when they jointly displayed their Canadian and American flags to reflect their love for both home countries. Leah's page stands firm in refusing to pass on hatred and ignorance, as is expressed patriotically through punched stars adhered to her focal photo.

Leah Blanco Williams, Rochester, New York

Supplies: Patterned papers (Creative Imaginations, Daisy D's, Hobby Lobby, Karen Foster Design, Mustard Moon); letter stamps (Leave Memories); folk art star punch (EK Success); acrylic paint

United We Stand

While Holle's husband was deployed with the Army, pouring herself into designing pages like this one helped keep her sanity intact and her hope alive. She printed the story of her time apart from her husband and their strengthening shared faith on manila paper attached to both the outside and inside a large handcut file folder. Holle used sepia-toned photos to mesh with the page overall and highlighted them with printed negative frames.

Holle Wiktorek, Reunion, Colorado

Supplies: Patterned paper (Flair Designs); letter stamps (Hero Arts, La Pluma); negative holders (Creative Imaginations); distress ink (Ranger); cardstock; stamping ink

Celebrate My Age

Carolyn stopped the sands of time long enough to pause and reflect upon the milestone of turning 30. She filled her page with joyful photos to create a festive tone in her layout. Lyric excerpts from a Tim McGraw song made for a fitting title, and Carolyn wrote additional thoughts on ribbon-adorned cards tucked behind her focal photo. The light springtime colors help convey her realization that turning 30 is just the beginning of her life and that "the best is yet to come!"

Carolyn Lontin, Highlands Ranch, Colorado
Photos: Rick Lontin, Highlands Ranch, Colorado

Supplies: Patterned papers (K & Company); textured cardstock (Bazzill); rub-on letters (Scrapworks); ribbons (May Arts); decorative paper clip (EK Success); photo turns (Making Memories); mini brads (SEI); black clock (Li'l Davis Designs); silk flowers (Wal-Mart); stamping ink

...Curly Girl

For years, Jenn tried to suppress her curls into submission. But after reading a book on the subject titled *Curly Girl*, by Lorraine Massey, she became inspired to release her own "inner curly girl" in this layout. To illustrate her "war of the ringlets," Jenn used photos from different hair-stages of life, converting them to black-and-white wallet size using image-editing software. She kept her focal photo in color to reveal her acceptance of the hair she's been blessed with. Jenn chose assorted patterned papers with lots of curves to help reflect the theme.

Jenn Brookover, San Antonio, Texas
Portrait Photo: Kyle Brookover,
San Antonio, Texas

Supplies: Patterned papers (Chatterbox, EK Success, Pebbles, SEI, 7 Gypsies); flower sticker (Meri Meri); ribbon, mailbox letters (Making Memories); letter stickers (Li'l Davis Designs); clip (Karen Foster Design); distress ink (Ranger); circle punch (Family Treasures); image-editing software (Adobe Photoshop); transparency

One Moment...

It took Kathy four-and-a-half years to muster up the courage to create a page to lament her sorrow and guilt over an accident that would haunt any mother's worst nightmare. Her journaling reveals a detailed account of her son's near drowning after coming across a forgotten mop bucket. Kathy used number stickers and a vellum clock element to preserve the exact moment her heart stood still in desperation. Image-editing software was used to alter the image of her son's striking gaze of forgiveness.

Kathy Fesmire, Athens, Tennessee

Supplies: Patterned papers (Anna Griffin, Chatterbox); vellum clock (DMD); ribbons (Offray); decorative brads, metal sheeting, rub-on letters (Making Memories); letter and number stickers (Chatterbox); letter stencil (Avery); image-editing software (Adobe Photoshop); clear acrylic spray (Krylon); cardstock; stamping ink; acrylic paint; embroidery thread; buttons

Sam

The peace and tranquility Samuel felt in this photo is reflected with soft, soothing colors and distressed patterns. The accompanying lyrics to a favorite hymn by Horatio Gates Spafford perfectly convey the sense of awe and relaxation. Samuel balanced the crisp lines of the photo in his page design by adding circle punches, round letter stickers and rounded bookmarks for a quality of softness.

Samuel Cole, Stillwater, Minnesota

Supplies: Patterned papers, ruler stickers, bookmarks, letter stickers, epoxy corner stickers, circle punch (EK Success); metal label holder (source unknown); text stamp (Hampton Art Stamps); cardstock; chalk; brads; stamping ink; sandpaper

Sweet Serenity

A prayer of serenity, placed beneath Amber's self-portrait, served as the inspiration for this layout. Her page has a quiet strength about it, featuring richly colored distressed patterns and sophisticated page elements, which help convey her acceptance of the feelings she has toward her body, attitude and overall self. The sleek ribbon accents and their accompanying attachments emphasize Amber's sense of style.

Amber McDonald, Las Vegas, Nevada

Supplies: Patterned paper (Basic Grey); ribbons (Michaels, Offray, SEI); metal ribbon charm, decorative brad, foam letter stamps (Making Memories); spiral paper clip, photo turns (7 Gypsies); crystal lacquer (Sakura Hobby Craft); acrylic paint

Thankful

Judith's page overflows with her life's blessings and the thankfulness she feels for each one. She stamped and handwrote her journaling on individual tags, defining in detail the ways her husband, children, friends, family, dog, work, house and passions are all so dear to her heart. A stitched canvas frame and printed twill elements lend nurturing warmth to the page while ribbons, stencils and title stones convey a sense of simplicity and beauty in the basics.

Judith Mara, Lancaster, Massachusetts
Photo: Dean DeChambeau,
Lancaster, Massachusetts

Supplies: Patterned papers (Autumn Leaves); canvas frame (www.treasurequest .com); chipboard stencil letter (Making Memories); printed twill (Creative Impressions); ribbon (7 Gypsies); polymer clay (Polyform Products); letter stamps (All Night Media, PSX Design); acrylic paint; stamping ink; sandpaper; staples

A Minivan Mom

The transition to "minivan mom" was not an easy one for Joanna, but one she now embraces and wouldn't trade for the world. To print her notebook paper-style journaling passage, she attached a sheet of composition paper to computer paper for ease in printing. Joanna based her color scheme around the color of her now-beloved van as well as around the tranquil blues in both photographs.

Joanna Bolick, Fletcher, North Carolina
Photos: Mark Bolick, Fletcher, North Carolina

Supplies: Patterned papers (Basic Grey, Chatterbox); image-editing software (Adobe Photoshop); composition paper

I believe...

in the goodness of humanity and that beauty lies within. That optimism is wisdom and spirituality is a guiding light. I believe in the power of words, in the withholding of rash judgment and that dreams are simply realities in the making. I believe in setting examples worthy of emulation. That strength of character is built upon sound principle. I believe in self-expression. In faith and kindness. I believe the best in life is still to come.

I don't like it when people call me "religious." True Christianity is mo__ that. It's more than a set of rules to live by. It's more than going to chur__ Sunday.

It's a relationship.

I'm still me. But Christ lives in me. He speaks to my heart through prayer. He speaks to me through His Word, the Bible. This does not mean I'm perfect.

I'm still human.

But I'm never alone. When I'm up, when I'm down, through my joys & struggles, He shares in them with me. He celebrates with my triumphs & holds me in my failures. He is always with me, even though I can't see Him with my eyes, I feel Him with my heart.

How do I know?

Faith. Pure & simple. When I was 16 years old I gave my life to Jesus to do with what He will. Not that my life has been perfect; like I said, I'm human. But He's proven Himself faithful time & time again. He leads me in the paths I should go & straightens me out when I stray.

What more could I want?

He doesn't promise riches or an easy life, but He does promise that there is nothing that I can't get through with His help. Christ is not a genie sent to __rant three wishes. But He is there for me. He's forgive me for my sins. And I __ spend eternity in heaven with Him.

"For I know the plans I have for you," declares the Lord, "plans to prosper you and not to harm you, plans to give you hope & a future." Jeremiah 29:11

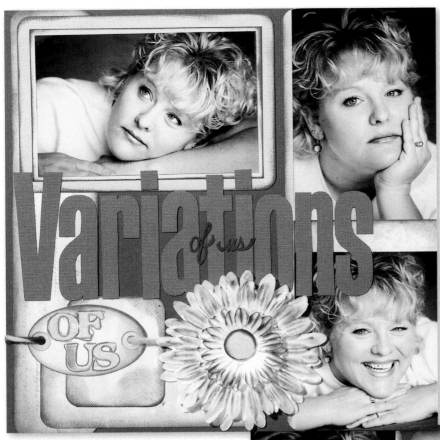

Variations of Us

Integrating variations of her own image into one design proved to be the perfect outlet for Cherie to express her thoughts on diversity in American culture. She used a multicolored strand of yarn to guide her color choices and blended the page elements together by inking all edges. The layout overall illustrates Cherie's belief that though each individual functions independently, we can work in harmony to create one beautiful, cohesive whole.

Cherie Ward, Colorado Springs, Colorado

Supplies: Patterned paper; round tag, letter stickers (Basic Grey); textured cardstocks (Bazzill); ribbons, fibers (Lion, Offray); letter stamps (Ma Vinci's Reliquary); silk flower; stamping ink

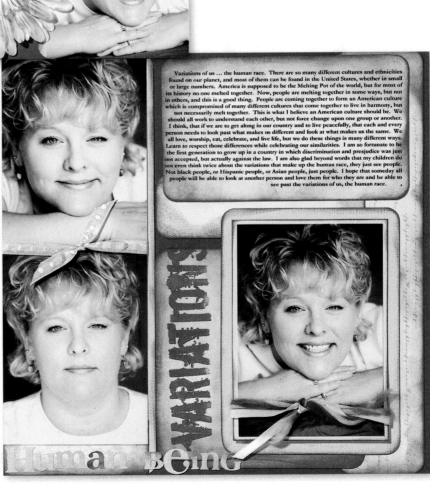

Variations of us ... the human race. There are so many different cultures and ethnicities found on our planet, and most of them can be found in the United States, whether in small or large numbers. America is supposed to be the Melting Pot of the world, but for most of its history no one melted together. Now, people are melting together in some ways, but not in others, and this is a good thing. People are coming together to form an American culture which is compromised of many different cultures that come together to live in harmony, but not necessarily melt together. This is what I believe an American culture should be. We should all work to understand each other, but not force change upon one group or another. I think, that if we are to get along in our country and to live peacefully, that each and every person needs to look past what makes us different and look at what makes us the same. We all love, worship, eat, celebrate, and live life, but we do these things many different ways. Learn to respect those differences while celebrating our similarities. I am so fortunate to be the first generation to grow up in a country in which discrimination and prejudice was just not accepted, but actually against the law. I am also glad beyond words that my children do not even think twice about the variations that make up the human race, they just see people. Not black people, or Hispanic people, or Asian people, just people. I hope that someday all people will be able to look at another person and love them for who they are and be able to see past the variations of us, the human race.

Beauty Lies Within

From Drama Queen at 17 to Beauty Queen at 30, Deborah proudly marches on to reign as queen of her house and herself. She used this layout to demonstrate how her idea of beauty has changed over the years and accented each image with a title-corresponding charm. The right page describes her journey to discover that beauty comes from within, and she artfully expresses it with a collage of textures, ephemera and words. An actual watch face provides the finishing touch, symbolic of the passage of time.

Deborah Conken, Riverside, California

Supplies: Patterned papers (Chatterbox, SEI); letter stencil, fabric tags, mini brad (Making Memories); acrylic letters (Heidi Grace Designs); rub-on letters (Chatterbox); ribbons (Making Memories, May Arts, Offray); metal charms (Provo Craft); watch face (found on eBay); button, decorative clip (Ek Success); epoxy word sticker (K & Company); fabric swatches (Jo-Ann Stores); mesh (Magic Mesh); label maker (Dymo); tissue paper; stamping inks; jewelry tag; rivet; sandpaper; acrylic paint; gloss medium

More Than a Belief...

Soft, warm colors provide a serene backdrop for Courtney's page that defines her way of life as a Christian. As her faith has always been an integral part of who she is, Courtney felt compelled to create a layout to express why. She incorporated big and bold chipboard letters into her title to emphasize the message behind her journaling which explains how Christianity is beyond a belief—and how it defines her through and through.

Courtney Walsh, Winnebago, Illinois

Supplies: Patterned papers, letter stickers, rub-on letters (Chatterbox); textured cardstock (Bazzill); brads (Making Memories); chipboard letters (Li'l Davis Designs); stamping ink

Be Aware of Your Beliefs

The belief system that Sharon has acquired with time and wisdom includes many shades of gray which is illustrated in her design through gray chalked edges, pewter accents and in the tones of her title and featured quote. Her journaling focuses on the importance of not judging people but rather trying to look for the beauty inside everyone. Sharon played up her quote with photos of flowers and paper flower accents.

Sharon Whitehead, Vernon,
British Columbia, Canada

Supplies: Textured cardstock (Bazzill); mesh (Magic Mesh); ribbon charms, metal letter tiles, paper flowers, snaps (Making Memories); chalk (Craf-T)

be aware of your beliefs

When I was a child I was a big ole tattletale, because I was always right. At 16, I believed the world was black and white. Everything was either right or wrong. No greys in my world. I was always gonna be right. I learned in time that the world is full of many shades of grey. Thank heaven my belief system now includes the thoughts expressed by the following quote -

"The only difference between a flower and a weed is a judgment."

I discovered it is so important to be aware of the power making a judgment has on your life. So often, in my youth, I made judgments without regard to their impact on my life or others. I admit, I was a bit judgmental...OK..."a lot" judgmental. I probably still am sometimes (nobody's perfect, right?) but I strive to remember those words and what they signify before I get on my judgment throne. My world revolves around gentler shades of grey these days. I now know that it's ok to admit to yourself that you're not always going to be right and to open yourself up to the other guys point of view. Now, that doesn't mean that you have to cave on your beliefs and adopt his. No siree, it just means that you can listen, truly listen, without a "but" on the tip of your tongue. I think for me that was the hardest part. So, always be aware of your beliefs, their impact on your life and others, and your power to change them.

My view

SAME gIrL.

STACEY MICHELLE DOUGLASS

imagine the possibilities...

I am still the same girl. But 34 years later, I live in a very different world. In 1970, I knew nothing of being a mom, paying bills, terrorists, the internet, child molesters, scrapbooking, peer pressure, HGTV...the good and the bad that are in my world today. I realize that many of those things existed, but they had not affected me yet. I was just so blissfully unaware of the days that would come, a little girl having an easy three-year-old life.

At the age of 37, I am wise enough to know that what life has brought me is what has made me who I am today, the hurts and the blessings. God has used the events and circumstances of my life to mold me into the person He created me to be. And He is not finished. But I am still the same girl.

Philippians 1:6
For I am confident of this very thing, that He who began a good work in you will perfect it until the day of Christ Jesus.

happy
1970

I Am Still the Same Girl

After 34 years, Stacey may have become introduced to the complexities of the adult world, but the same little girl captured in her page's photo, complete with her unwavering faith, still exists inside. Stacey's use of green conjures notions of newness, growth and innocence that are perfect for her page theme. A multimedia title treatment, paint chip and ribbon accents keep the layout youthful and fun.

Stacey Kingman, Ellsworth, Illinois
Photo: Jo Douglass, Fulshear, Texas

Supplies: Textured cardstocks (Bazzill); dog tags (Chronicle Books); colored brads, metal frame, rub-on words (Making Memories); ribbon (Li'l Davis Designs); label maker (Dymo); acrylic flowers, acrylic word (KI Memories); letter stickers (Doodlebug Design); acrylic paint; paint chip

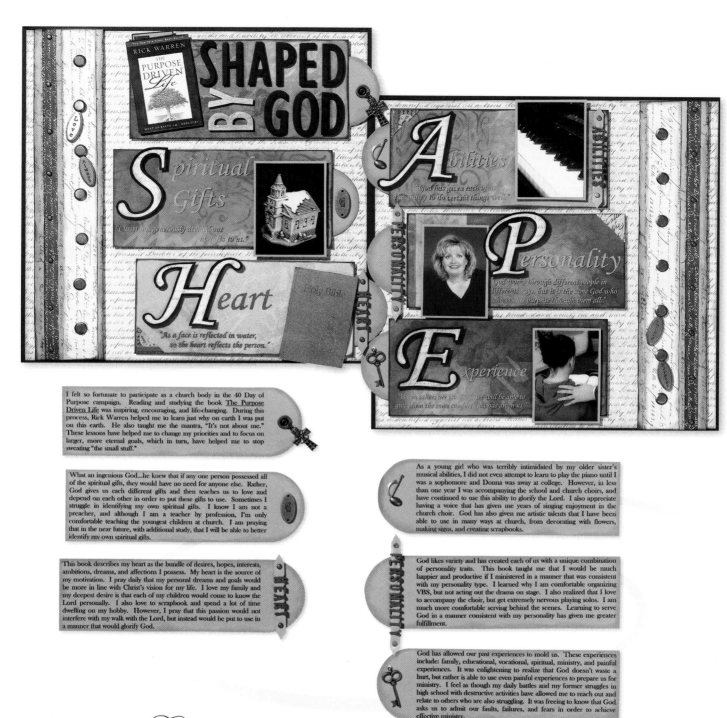

Shaped by God

After going through the book *The Purpose Driven Life* by Rick Warren, Denise was inspired to document its lasting impression. She employed acrostic-style journaling by using each letter of the word "Shape" to emphasize a different focus from the book. She then printed each subheading on a transparency which was then heat embossed. Each focus has a separate block with a decorative pullout tag that shares the ways God has shaped Denise in each area. Depth and dimension were achieved through self-adhesive foam spacers.

Denise Tucker, Versailles, Indiana
Portrait Photo: The Picture People, Florence, Kentucky

Supplies: Patterned papers (7 Gypsies, Crafter's Workshop, Rusty Pickle); cardstock (Rusty Pickle); wooden letters (Wal-Mart); zipper pulls (Junkitz); letter slides (Karen Foster Design); epoxy corners (EK Success); cross charm (Sulyn Industries); key charm (Boutique Trims); note charm (source unknown); large brads (All My Memories); mini brads (Artchix Studio); metallic paint pen (Krylon); rivet (Chatterbox); distress ink (Ranger)

I Believe in Journals

Lisa uses journaling as a means of sifting and sorting through her thoughts on life. She wanted to capture the essence of her late-night writing sessions by incorporating the candles she burns as part of her writing ritual. To do so, she melted beeswax and dipped her title, silk flowers and an actual journal excerpt into the wax for a translucent effect. To keep her journaling from getting lost against the patterned paper background, Lisa painted a layer of wax directly onto the back of the printed transparency.

Lisa Dixon, East Brunswick, New Jersey

Supplies: Patterned paper, large monogram letter, letter stickers, tag (Basic Grey); letter tiles (Colorbök); rub-on letters, mini brads (Making Memories); ribbon (May Arts); coated linen thread (Scrapworks); distress ink (Ranger); beeswax; silk flowers; notebook paper; sandpaper; transparency

Testimony

Christine's inspirational testimony of how she found and embraced her faith is neatly bound in a journaling booklet secured to her page with an elastic band. Inside the paint-stamped cardstock pages, Christine reflects on the events of her life-altering personal journey. Layered and distressed patterned papers, stamped transparencies and ornate painted page elements combine beautifully with Christine's uplifting photo.

Christine Brown, Hanover, Minnesota

Supplies: Patterned papers (Colorbök, Memories in the Making, Paper Loft); foam alphabet and decorative stamps, label holder, alphabet charms, molding accents, corners, definition sticker (Making Memories); stamps (PSX Design); elastic cord (7 Gypsies); decorative stick pin (EK Success); ribbon; stamping ink; acrylic paint; cardstock

I Believe

For this layout encompassing the heart of Angie's faith, she created decorative strips and text boxes for each line of a Rich Mullins song based upon the Apostles' Creed. The staggered strips provide a tranquil, sturdy feel to her page with the negative spaces playing a critical role in the design. Ornate crosses and metal accents lend a majestic flair and draw attention to her patterned papers.

Angie Head, Friendswood, Texas

Supplies: Patterned papers (Crossed Paths); fabric tags (Frazzles); decorative photo corners (Karen Foster Design); metal crosses (Card Connection); decorative staples (EK Success); metal embellishments (Card Connection, Karen Foster Design)

Note to self

If you want to pass along certain values and moral lessons to your loved ones you feel are especially important, consider writing an "ethical will." Ethical wills are a way of sharing your values, wisdom, forgiveness, hopes and dreams with your family, friends and community. Ethical wills can be free-form or specifically structured. They may take the form of a letter to your child or a future descendant, or may simply be a list of lessons and guidance you wish to pass on. In committing your personal wisdom to paper, nothing will be left unsaid. Use these prompts to get started:

• What advice would you give someone on living a good and moral life?

• What have you learned from your parents and/or grandparents?

• What are your priorities in life?

• What do you regret doing, or not doing?

• What has been left unsaid?

Believe

After seeing a movie that changed her life, Mel Gibson's *The Passion of the Christ*, Christie felt compelled to document the striking experience in a scrapbook page. Referring to particular scenes that most touched her, Christie journaled her feelings and the overall emotional and spiritual impact of the film. A simple title, dramatic crimson colors, distressed papers and the absence of photos keep the focus on Christie's experience. Tucked behind a printed ribbon are the actual ticket stubs accented by a die-cut Christian fish symbol.

Christie Wildes, Gainesville, Florida

Supplies: Patterned paper (Li'l Davis Designs); cardstock (Bazzill); hinge, washer, ribbon, ribbon charm, definition sticker, buttons (Making Memories); die-cut fish (Ek Success); solvent ink (Tsukineko); thread; ticket stubs

I Believe in God

Wanting to pass on her belief that each child is special and unique, Heidi shares a story with her daughters that her grandmother once told her—that God created each of us with one-of-a-kind cookie cutters and poked our stomachs Pillsbury-style to see if we were "done"—hence our belly buttons! The circular photo frames continue the theme throughout while buttons and stitching lend a homespun touch of a mother's love to the page. Heidi numbered her own little "cookies" in order, adding initial accents to each.

Heidi Schueller, Waukesha, Wisconsin

Supplies: Patterned paper (Flair Designs); cardstock (Chatterbox); flower brads, letter charms (Jo-Ann Stores); cork paper, buttons (Magic Scraps); die-cut letters, tag, flower punches (Sizzix); ribbon (Michaels); fibers (Timeless Touches); mini safety pin (Making Memories); number stencil (Target); letter stamps (Hero Arts, PSX Design); distress ink (Ranger); transparency

I Believe

Here Valerie elegantly incorporated the faith by which she lives into a scrapbook page. She kept the layout simple to share in a precise and purposeful way the basic truths she adheres to. Silver embossing powder pulls the eye across the page, highlighting one of several symbolic patterned papers present in the design.

Valerie Barton, Flowood, Mississippi

Supplies: Patterned paper, circle tag (Crossed Paths); metal word charm, silk flowers, foam letter stamps (Making Memories); leaf stamp (Hero Arts); leaf clips (Scrappin' Extras); watch face (source unknown); keyhole accent (Li'l Davis Designs); mini brads (American Tag Co.); watermark ink (Tsukineko); staples; vellum; ribbon; embossing powder; acrylic paint

I Believe...

Heather recognizes that a person's tongue can be a double-edged sword and created this photoless layout to share her thoughts on the subject. Her journaling reveals her own beliefs behind the words she shares with others in order to impact the world for the better. A variety of colors in the title brings a fresh and positive spin to the thematically black-and-white journaling section while reflecting the patterned paper echoed in the circle-shape accents.

Heather Preckel, Swannanoa,
North Carolina

Supplies: Patterned papers (Basic Grey, 7 Gypsies); textured cardstock (AC Moore); ribbon (May Arts); letter stickers (American Crafts); mini brad (Making Memories); silk flower (Prima); stamping ink

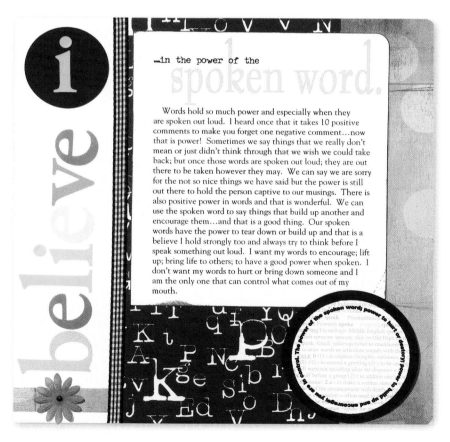

At 29 and 3/4

As Teri approached 30, she created this self page to capture her beliefs at this stage in life. She thought it would be interesting to look back at this page in her senior years to see if these thoughts still hold true for her. Each belief was printed on computer paper, cut into strips and folded over with wire inside to look like twist ties. She sealed each strip, allowed it to dry and then twisted the ends.

Teri Anderson, Vancouver, Washington

Supplies: Patterned paper, index tab sticker, flower, square tags, ribbon (SEI); date stamp (Staples); chalk ink (Clearsnap); wire; staples; stamping ink

Key to a Fulfilled Life

The doors to Pamela's heart are opened in this triptych-style layout which highlights her greatest blessings. A decorative tag on the front expresses her love for God, family and nature while an overlapping tag journals a small introduction to the inner workings of her design. Both sides of the front open to reveal artistic celebrations for her salvation, creation and relations. She inked the edges of each section, as well as vellum quotes from a favorite hymn and Scripture.

Pamela James, Ventura, California
Photos: Thom James, Ventura, California

Supplies: Patterned paper (Autumn Leaves); textured cardstock (Bazzill); family and friends medallion (K & Company); brass key (Boutique Trims); rectangular frame (Michaels); square frame, oval tags (Making Memories); gold decorative corners (Magic Scraps); skeleton leaves (Gartner Studios); decorative paper clips (Scrapworks); silk ribbon; brads; vellum; transparency; silk flowers; acrylic paint; varnish; stamping ink

Hope & Faith

Gina designed this page as a reminder of the strength and peace that come from her personal faith even in times of great difficulty. She created this layout as she prepared to visit her aging mother far away, whom she had not seen in 13 years. The soft, pretty pinks played against browns lend a lightness and hopefulness to her somber subject. Gina handcut her title letters and embellished her journaling with ribbons in celebration of the fact that she no longer sheds tears of sorrow, but rather tears of hope.

Gina Regala, San Jose, California

Supplies: Patterned papers (Autumn Leaves, EK Success); textured cardstock (Bazzill); ribbon (May Arts); craft knife

Love Letters to My Maker

A mini book adhered to the upper right of Courtney's layout gives inspirational insight into the black-and-white images she chose for this page. Her journaling book reveals a love letter to God in which she expresses her heartfelt love and appreciation for knowing her heart's desires even before she recognized them herself. Soft fabrics, slightly distressed patterned paper, flowers and bows lend softness and a feminine, nurturing quality to the page.

Courtney Walsh, Winnebago, Illinois

Supplies: Patterned paper (Chatterbox, Karen Foster Design); textured cardstock (Bazzill); ribbon (Offray); lace, key charm (EK Success); rivets (Chatterbox); letter stamps (PSX Design); foam letter stamps, round metal label holder, word washer, staples (Making Memories); fabric (Wendy Bellisimo); photo corners (Pioneer); stamping ink; acrylic paint; embroidery floss; eyelets

I know...

the best lessons are seldom easily learned. That love is infinite, time is relentless and at the end of even the darkest of tunnels awaits the light. I know that mistakes are best measured by the ways they are redeemed. That a hearty dosage of laughter often is the best medicine. I know that attitude is a choice. That perspective transcends vision. I know that wisdom of the heart is meant to be passed on.

commitment

SENS

STUBBORN

determination

What can I be certain of in my life? The love I feel and receive from my family, that the sky is blue and that I can never have too much patterned paper. As each year passes I think I have it all figured out. Then I realize there is no true certainty. I was certain my heart was not big enough to love my husband AND my family. Then our son was born— which proved that the heart's ability to love is endless. I was certain fulfillment would only come via a career. Then I became a stay-at-home Mom and now fulfillment comes each day as I watch my son flourish. Who would have guessed that all of this uncertainty would result in so much happiness? I never expect and always be thankful—this I know!

march 2005

Reflection

When Sheryl's mother passed away, she sadly realized there was so much more she wanted to know about her beliefs, thoughts and dreams. In turn, she created this page for her own daughter featuring her "Sheryl-isms"—lessons learned and taught—printed inside a folded paper envelope. Each tidbit of wisdom represents Sheryl's reflections on life. Clock hands and small mirror tiles provide symbolic and artful page additions.

Sheryl DeBuhr, Memphis, Tennessee
Photos: Steve DeBuhr, Memphis, Tennessee

Supplies: Patterned paper (Basic Grey); foam letter stamps, mini brads, date stamp (Making Memories); photo turns (7 Gypsies); clock hands (Walnut Hollow), leather tie-ups (EK Success); mirror tiles (Crafts Etc.); distress ink (Ranger); spray paint; brads

What I Know...

Scrapbooking is more than just a hobby to Kimberly—it's an extension of who she is and a means by which she has has cultivated a garden of friendships. This layout celebrates these recently-bloomed relationships in Kimberly's life on tags that reveal the way each individual has affected Kimberly's art. Tactile "tag toppers" blend into the patterned paper and photo, providing a bouquet of collected wisdom from friendships that continue to grow.

Kimberly Kesti, Phoenix, Arizona

Supplies: Patterned papers (Basic Grey, Junkitz); textured cardstock (Bazzill); buttons, fabric (Junkitz); ribbons (May Arts); twill (Creek Bank Creations); silk flower; stamping ink

Sweet Tea

Symbols come in all shapes and sizes, and for Julie, gathering with loved ones looks like a pitcher of tea. She created this page to demonstrate how one basic item, like this pitcher, can have so much meaning. Her patterns and colors convey a relaxed, comfortable charm, much like the association she has with the welcoming image of the pitcher and the conversations that always surround it.

Julie Johnson, Seabrook, Texas

Flow Dont Force

Learning to gently go with the flow rather than force problems into submission was a lesson Elizabeth learned through a hobby. She created this page as a reminder of how she was able to grasp an enlightening concept through a small and mundane activity—sorting through a tangled mess of yarn. She knotted the ribbons on her page, adding a vibrant sense of whimsy as well as a visual reminder to loosen up and work with her problems rather than compound them.

Elizabeth Ruuska, Rensselaer, Indiana

Supplies: Patterned papers (Junkitz); chipboard letters (Li'l Davis Designs); ribbons (Doodlebug Design, May Arts); letter page pebbles (Junkitz)

An Open Mind

After reading harsh criticism about the types of scrapbook pages published in magazines, Bay designed this layout as a place to vent her own philosophy on the art of scrapbooking. She wrestles with the question of whether most pages depict reality or fiction, with the conclusion that they all contain meaningful reflections of the individual when viewed with an open mind. For her own creation, she combined various images of herself with altered photos and ephemera that have stories of their own.

Bay Loftis, Philadelphia, Tennessee

Supplies: Textured and patterned cardstocks, etched acrylic block, mini compass, ribbon (Club Scrap); die-cut letters (Accu-Cut); watch crystal (Jest Charming); alcohol inks (Ranger); stamping inks; key; wax wine seal; seed beads; lock of hair

What is real? What is fake? When do the pages in my scrapbook reflect **real life**, and when are they just a **façade** of what I wish my life were like?

Is my scrapbook less valid, less worthy because I labor over each page as if it were a **masterpiece** that I'll sell to a wealthy patron? Doesn't it matter that no benefactor is going to sponsor my work, or that I'll **never get rich making layouts?**

I *expect* non-artists to sniff and scoff and turn up their noses at my work. I'm not surprised when an acquaintance says, **"You have too much time on your hands."** I've been involved in the arts my entire life, and I've heard that refrain so often that I honestly don't anticipate acceptance from outsiders. In fact, I'm proud of my stubborn grasp on **my individuality.**

But when fellow scrapbookers belittle my work on the basis that I spend extra time on my layouts, it hurts. **It hurts.** They say that I don't make my layouts for myself, and they claim superiority to me because they're doing it "to get it done for history."

They disparage pages with photos that they claim are bogus, based on the fact that I actually **stopped and thought** a little about the composition of the frame and the lighting before I snapped the shutter. They deride layouts with **one big picture**, never minding the fact that I rarely take more than one picture that's focused well enough to put on a layout. If you can't tell who the subject is, why use the picture?

For those who say carefully composed photos are fake, I tell you this: **I don't have enough pictures of my parents**, posed or candid. And my father was a prolific, talented, amateur photographer. After his death thirty years ago, we began to realize that there aren't many pictures of him except for his early self-portraits. The majority of the pictures of my mother are from her youth, when I didn't know her.

Those photos are not only posed, most of them were assigned in class and dealt more with **capturing light** and shadow than in memorializing my parents. Are they any **less** beloved because they were posed? No.

Vehemently, strongly, **profoundly – *no***, they are more treasured because they're in them, regardless of the purpose behind the use of film and developing fluid and paper. They are all I have left of them, and I love every single one. I only **wish** there were more.

I'm a truly ungifted photographer. If I had to rely on my bad, candid snapshots for my scrapbooks, no one would ever know what my children look like, or **what I look like, or** where we were when we held Woodrow's 12th birthday party. I'm **grateful** every day for the little digital camera that Wesley and Amy gave me last summer, because finally I'm getting pictures that look a little more like the pictures I see **in my head.**

In fifty years, **when I'm not here**, my children and grandchildren will be able to look through my scrapbooks, read what I wrote, and see *some* of what I see today. If they **look beyond** the pictures and the paper, the techniques and the trimmings, **they'll see my soul.**

Sure, it isn't realistic. Souls never are; they're **ephemeral**, even if they're posed and labored over for hours on end. Every single page holds my soul, **flawed** but striving for impossible perfection, seeking the **truth** and telling poetic fictions, longing to reveal the unknowable and **glossing** over reality.

By the way, in the interest of complete honesty, the photos on these pages are both fake and real.

The black-and-white headshots are altered from professional negatives that I bought for my stage resumé. I wouldn't have bought them if I didn't **see myself in them.**

And the color pictures? Emily took them with my simple, inexpensive camera. All I had to do was sit still and let this **untrained**, teenaged photography enthusiast wield her craft. If she sees me in them, then we have both succeeded.

I don't know much, but I do know this: Even if some individual parts are staged, **every scrapbook is real** on some level. It just takes an open mind to see it.

I Know...

The carefree, funky feel of Danielle's page captures her belief in the power of a relaxed lease on life. Her journaling illustrates how some of the best things can happen when you aren't trying to make them happen and that it helps to learn to go with the flow. For a fun look and texture, Danielle dry-embossed flowers using a flower template—debossing, embossing, then debossing the shape again. She then sanded the raised edges to expose the white core in the cardstock. Rounded corners reflect the relaxed attitude of this playful page.

Danielle Thompson, Tucker, Georgia

Supplies: Patterned papers (American Traditional Designs, Anna Griffin); textured cardstock (Bazzill); letter stickers (Doodlebug Design, Li'l Davis Designs); embossing template (Lasting Impressions); felt flower (Cost Plus World Market); ribbon (Offray); image-editing software (Adobe Photoshop); pom-pom trim (antique market find); pen; corner rounder

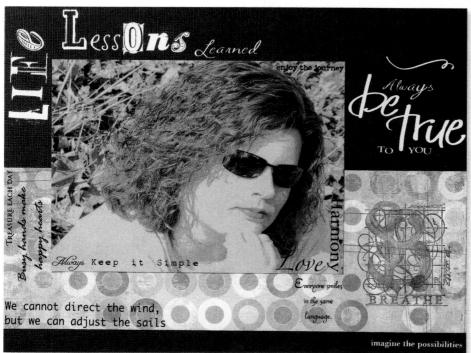

**Becky Thompson,
Fruitland, Idaho
Photo: Amy Brown,
Payette, Idaho**

Supplies: Patterned paper (Basic Grey); textured cardstock (Bazzill); letter stamp (Stampers Anonymous); rub-on letters and words (Chatterbox, C-Thru Ruler, Making Memories, Provo Craft); image-editing software (Adobe Photoshop); distress ink (Ranger)

Life Lessons Learned

With age comes wisdom, and Becky used this page as an outlet for showcasing the words she believes in and lives by. The process was made simple by combining key words and sentimental rub-on letters that perfectly capture her life philosophy. She altered her photograph with image-editing software to create a dreamy, surreal effect to perfectly complement the hues of her patterned paper.

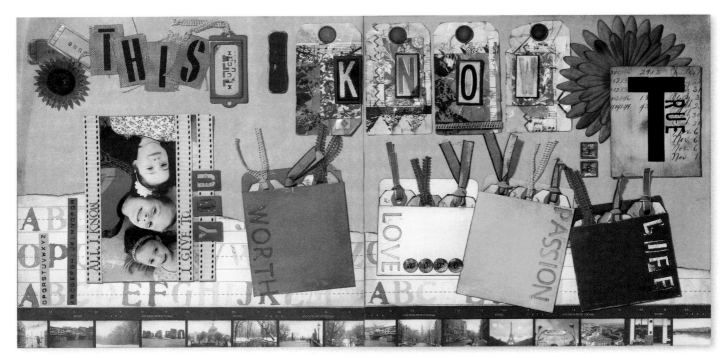

This Much I Know Is *True*...

In this layout, Colleen passes along treasured wisdom to her children straight from her heart as a mother. Colleen created pockets for the life elements of Worth, Love, Passion and Life, and placed three tags inside each. The journaling tags are inscribed with her personal convictions toward each topic. Red flower accents and alphabet paper keep the page lighthearted and vibrant, and a multimedia title treatment adds instant visual appeal.

Colleen Macdonald, Winthrop, Australia

Supplies: Patterned papers (Li'l Davis Designs, Me & My Big Ideas, Stamp It); cardstock letter stickers (Paper Loft); letter stamps (Hero Arts); ribbon (Lincraft); rub-on letters; fabric letters, raffle ticket stickers, metal label holders, metal memorabilia, epoxy letters, cardstock tag stickers, metal stencil letters (Li'l Davis Designs); library cards (Boxer Scrapbook Productions, Li'l Davis Designs); solvent ink (Tsukineko); small shipping tags; embossing powder; stamping inks

Note to self

Complete these statements:

- I am convinced...
- Everyone should...
- I hope my children always...

- I will never...
- I know for sure that love...
- The best way to deal with change is...
- To be happy, you need...

- The hardest thing to learn in life is...
- To live a balanced life you must...
- Success isn't...
- Worry will make you...

I Know That I Can Achieve *Anything* I Set My Mind To

Confident she can accomplish whatever she puts her mind to, Suzy is determined to help her children find that same sense of inner strength. She made this layout a success by turning her personal mantra into a title, placing rub-on letters onto cardstock that were then cut into fun shapes and enhanced with a glaze for an epoxylike effect. A ribbon-adorned journaling block elaborates upon the root of Suzy's conviction.

Suzy West, Fremont, California

Supplies: Patterned papers (Keeping Memories Alive); textured cardstock (Bazzill); rub-on letters (K & Company); fabric letters (Making Memories); ribbons (Offray); dimensional adhesive (Ranger); transparency; silk flowers

What *Happy* Looks Like

Leah celebrates her conviction and awareness that being an individual who makes her own choices is what true success looks like. Though the path she chose to venture in life may prompt judgment by some of her peers, the joy on her face in the photograph sings praises to the road less traveled. She listed her vital statistics in separate "factoid" boxes, with directive lines lending order to the arrangement and helping to illuminate her face.

Leah Blanco Williams, Rochester, New York

Supplies: Patterned papers (Basic Grey, KI Memories); cardstock; stamping ink

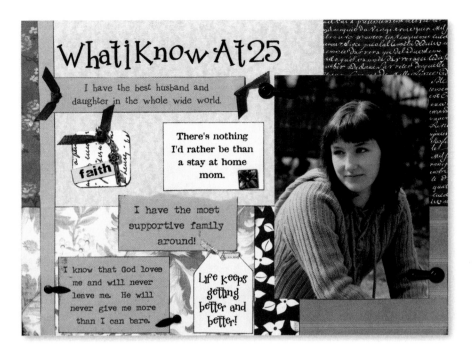

What I Know at 25

Maria used this layout as a keepsake of what life has taught her at age 25. She made separate tags for the things she holds dear and true to her heart, embellishing them with charms, ribbons and photo turns. Her collage of background papers gives a joyful quality to the page in this coming-of-age celebration of the important things in life.

Maria Burke, Steinbach, Manitoba, Canada
Photo: Howard Doerksen, Steinbach, Manitoba, Canada

Supplies: Patterned papers (Anna Griffin, Chatterbox, Frances Meyer, 7 Gypsies); script tag (DMD); photo turns (7 Gypsies); ribbon (Offray); key charm (Michaels); decorative flower brad, mini brads (Making Memories); cardstock

Moderation

Exhausted and frustrated with the struggle of fending off unwanted pounds, Diana discovered the key to a healthy lifestyle through the simple but profound process of moderation. This layout celebrates both Diana's physical accomplishment and emotional triumph. To remind her of just how far she's come, Diana tucked a "note to self" inside the stitched side-pocket which she reads for motivation at times when her resolve is tested. For an authentic perspective, she used an actual view from the scale as her featured image.

Diana Graham, Barrington, Illinois

Supplies: Patterned paper, library tab (7 Gypsies); die-cut letter "A," copper brads, ledger paper (Making Memories); definition file tab (Autumn Leaves); chipboard letters (Li'l Davis Designs); metal label holder (Creative Imaginations); decorative clip (EK Success); letter stickers, envelope (Chatterbox); ribbon (Offray); fabric photo corner (source unknown); dog tags; staples; cardstock

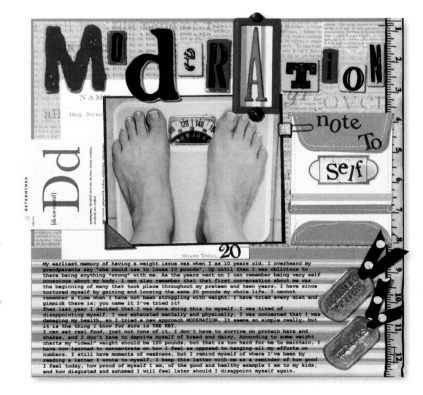

Dear self,
If you are reading this you may be needing a boost. I am here to remind you that you have been off this rollercoaster for some time now and don't want to get back on. You are feeling and looking so good. Your clothes fit, you don't have to wear your "fat" jeans! Think of how hard you have worked on working out; the soreness, the RESULTS of your hard work! If you are going to indulge go ahead, but don't let it send you to the DARK SIDE! Be good to yourself, love yourself, and take care of yourself. Do it for you, do it for the kids.
   LoVE your
   BETTER SELF

What I Know For Sure

Trudy's sophisticated spread muses on how time, faith and perseverance reveal the silver lining on even the darkest of clouds, making for a better today. Fabric labels boast uplifting sentiments while a series of sepia photos capture expressions reflected in the emotions detailed in her three journaling elements. Rich colors and feminine accents speak perfectly to Trudy's page theme of being a strong woman.

Trudy Sigurdson, Victoria, British Columbia, Canada

Supplies: Patterned papers (Basic Grey, Designs By Reminisce); metal accents (Karen Foster Design); square buttons (source unknown); ribbon (Creative Impressions); fabric labels (Me & My Big Ideas); walnut ink (7 Gypsies); letter stamps (EK Success); date stamp (Memories in the Making); flower stamp (Hero Arts); distress ink (Ranger); cotton lace; silk flowers

I have had many life experiences that at the time I would have rather not gone through. But now I look back at them all as valuable learning experiences, something that has made me the person that I am today and for that I am grateful. I now know that God only gives us what he knows we can handle and that we shouldn't question why something happens to us because the reason may

not be clear to us for along time but it will eventually make sense. Through my painful divorce and a bitter court case I now know that I am stronger than I ever gave myself credit for. I can be self sufficient and provide for my children on my own. I can stand up for myself and not let others walk all over me and I can say "no" if I don't want to do something or if I don't agree.

My opinion does matter and I do have a voice. I must never loose faith and work hard to accomplish what I want to in life and if I do these things, I will be able to reach all of my goals. Every cloud really does have a silver lining, it just might not be in the way we were hoping for, but it is there and we must never question or loose sight of that. This I know for sure. March 2005

Kelli Noto,
Centennial, Colorado
Photo: Bobbie Smith,
Centennial, Colorado

Supplies: Patterned papers, wooden frames (Chatterbox); die-cut letters (QuicKutz)

Lessons *Learned* From My Dad

Kelli attributes her values, morals and sound personal choices to her dad and pays tribute to his influence on this layout. She used the left border to showcase black-and-white photos of her father in younger years, then featured a current image of the two of them together on the right. Playful wooden frame accents lend a nostalgic element to the design which boasts a combination of childhood charm and masculine strength.

A *Real* Live Woman

Jodi found that the song "Real Live Woman" by Trisha Yearwood sings straight to her soul with words that echo her own acceptance and appreciation for who she is and what her life is all about. Tucked inside Jodi's journaling pocket is a pullout, paint-treated transparency printed with the lyrics. Her photo expresses confidence and contentment and resonates with the timeless colors and patterns in her design—a combination of femininity and strength.

Jodi Amidei, Memory Makers Books
Photo: Torrey Scott, Thornton, Colorado

Supplies: Patterned papers (Anna Griffin, Chatterbox, K & Company); mini eyelets (Making Memories); ribbon (Offray); buckle, acrylic letters (Paper Studio); corner rounders (EK Success); transparency (Grafix); silk flower; acrylic paint

I am not a political person. The most political thing I do is watch The West Wing on Wednesday nights. I don't like to talk politics, it is just such a personal thing. Whenever people discuss politics, it usually ends up as an argument and no one really listens to each other. I avoid those political exchanges and remind myself of the power I own – my vote. I lost 8 years of voting power to youth and ignorance. When I was 26 years old I realized the power of one vote and so began my commitment to vote in each and every election. I wear my little red sticker like a badge of honor.

The *Power* of One

At age 26, Jodi recognized the power of one vote and vowed to change her politically disinterested ways. She made a commitment to vote in every election and made this page as a tribute to her conviction. Jodi printed her title and a screened-back image of her voting sticker directly onto the background. Red, white and blue cut cardstock strips and punches add patriotism and depth. An actual voting sticker topped with ribbon provides the perfect finishing touch.

Jodi Heinen, Sartell, Minnesota
Photo: Jordan Heinen, Sartell, Minnesota

Supplies: Textured cardstock (Bazzill); ribbon (Wal-Mart); page pebble (Creative Imaginations); circle punch (Marvy); brads

What I *Know* @ 32

The best of both artistic worlds land lightheartedly on Susan's 8 x 8" design that shares her life lessons learned thus far. This computer-generated page is given added spark and spunk through butterfly transparencies and a tape measure border. An enlarged scan of Susan's signature flows across her layout, as do words of wisdom for an insightful and overall playful approach.

Susan Cyrus, Broken Arrow, Oklahoma

Supplies: Butterfly transparencies (Design Originals); tape measure paper (7 Gypsies); image-editing software (Adobe Photoshop)

what **i** know @ 32

People who say, "This too shall pass," are probably right. But you'll want to smack them in the head before it passes.

INVEST IN A GOOD CAMERA AND LEARN HOW TO USE IT. YOU WON'T REGRET IT.

Use sunscreen. :-)

YOU WILL NEVER HAVE AS MUCH DISCRETIONARY INCOME AS YOU DO IN YOUR TEENS AND TWENTIES. LEARN TO SAVE IT WHILE TIME IS ON YOUR SIDE.

Finding the right person makes all the difference.

I Aspire...

to explore and express my creative potential. To welcome new beginnings and changes with confidence and hope. I aspire to achieve my healthiest, happiest and most authentic self. To recognize ways I can improve through goals and resolutions. I aspire to surpass my own greatest expectations. To seek out new adventures. To parent with grace. I aspire to live my life without regrets, apologies or excuses.

In my life, I always thought about having a career, making lots of money, living in a big house with a swimming pool, and having three kids. These were my goals in life. I wanted to be married by the time I was 25, buy my first house by 27, and have my first child by 30. I was very driven, and accomplished many of them.

After Hayden was born, my goals changed. I didn't care about the big house, the money, my dream car. I didn't care about my 401K. All I cared about was making sure to kiss my husband and child every morning, to laugh and play, to stay up late and watch movies, to make special snacks.

[My] goals now are small and to some[,] [worth]less, but to me, priceless. My [one] goal is to make sure Hayden [looks] back and say "I had the best [...]. Everything else can wait. [My goa]l is to make tomorrow [better th]an today.

in my life

... I'm pretty sure that this is going to be a great year!

2005 great expectations

2005 Great Expectations

Deb entered the new year knowing there were beautiful scrapbook designs just waiting to spring from her colorful array of supplies. She carried the fun and playful feel of her photographs into her journaling, highlighting the words closely associated with her creations-to-be. A bold handcut paper flower accent adds instant whimsy while a multifont title spanning both pages provides powerful visual punch.

Deb Perry, Newport News, Virginia

Supplies: Number and letter stickers (American Crafts); word stickers (K & Company); acrylic gem (EK Success); pen; thread; cardstock

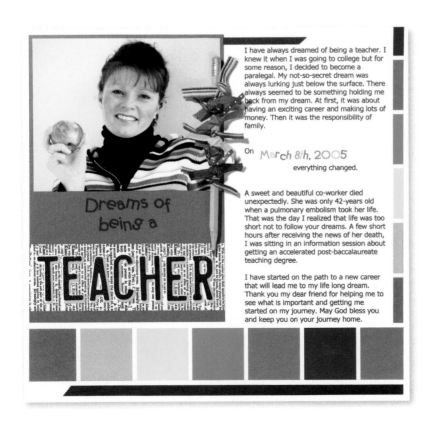

I have always dreamed of being a teacher. I knew it when I was going to college but for some reason, I decided to become a paralegal. My not-so-secret dream was always lurking just below the surface. There always seemed to be something holding me back from my dream. At first, it was about having an exciting career and making lots of money. Then it was the responsibility of family.

On March 8th, 2005 everything changed.

A sweet and beautiful co-worker died unexpectedly. She was only 42-years old when a pulmonary embolism took her life. That was the day I realized that life was too short not to follow your dreams. A few short hours after receiving the news of her death, I was sitting in an information session about getting an accelerated post-baccalaureate teaching degree.

I have started on the path to a new career that will lead me to my life long dream. Thank you my dear friend for helping me to see what is important and getting me started on my journey. May God bless you and keep you on your journey home.

Dreams of Being A Teacher

Abruptly reminded of the brevity of life, Jodi felt compelled not to wait another day to fulfill a long-postponed dream: to become a teacher. Immediately following the untimely passing of a colleague, Jodi got to work putting the wheels in motion to realize her goal. Her use of bright, happy colors looks as exciting as a fresh new box of crayons, and a decorated Number 2 pencil adds a sense of schoolhouse sparkle.

Jodi Heinen, Sartell, Minnesota

Supplies: Patterned paper (7 Gypsies); textured cardstock (Bazzill); letter stickers (Sticker Studio); paint strips (PM Designs); cardstock; ribbon

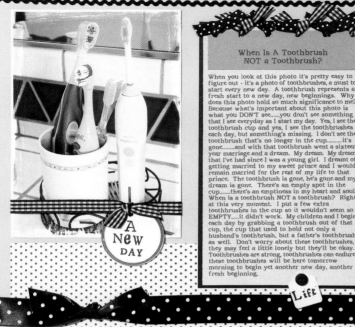

NEW BEGINNINGS

When Is A Toothbrush NOT a Toothbrush?

When you look at this photo it's pretty easy to figure out - it's a photo of toothbrushes, a must to start every new day. A toothbrush represents a fresh start to a new day, new beginnings. Why does this photo hold so much significance to me? Because what's important about this photo is what you DON'T see......you don't see something that I see everyday as I start my day. Yes, I see the toothbrush cup and yes, I see the toothbrushes each day, but something's missing. I don't see the toothbrush that's no longer in the cup.........it's gone........and with that toothbrush went a sixteen year marriage and a dream. My dream. My dream that I've had since I was a young girl. I dreamt of getting married to my sweet prince and I would remain married for the rest of my life to that prince. The toothbrush is gone, he's gone and my dream is gone. There's an empty spot in the cup.......there's an emptiness in my heart and soul. When is a toothbrush NOT a toothbrush? Right at this very moment. I put a few extra toothbrushes in the cup so it wouldn't seem so EMPTY.....it didn't work. My children and I begin each day by grabbing a toothbrush out of that cup, the cup that used to hold not only a husband's toothbrush, but a father's toothbrush as well. Don't worry about these toothbrushes, they may feel a little lonely but they'll be okay. Toothbrushes are strong, toothbrushes can endure, these toothbrushes will be here tomorrow morning to begin yet another new day, another fresh beginning.

A NEW DAY

Lift

New Beginnings

To help her through the grieving process of a divorce, Polly got her creative groove back and focused on a new day in her life. Her journaling explains the photo of toothbrushes in a cup—a familiar image that greets her and her children each day. Now, after 16 years, the toothbrushes are one less in number. Polly's bitter-sweet emotions are offset with bright, upbeat colors and festive prints. The journaling element lifts to reveal photos that represent the changing dynamic of her family and the smiles that still shine on each face.

Polly McMillan, Bullhead City, Arizona

Supplies: Patterned paper (Colorbök); textured cardstock (Bazzill); ribbon (Offray); rickrack (Wrights); tags (Avery); letter stamps (PSX Design)

Dream Catcher

This page was the first for Erin in a hopeful series of time capsules that she intends to update each year. She divided her dreams and goals into categories and stitched each pocket into place. She then wrote her ambitions for the year on separate tags, pocketing each into its respective category. Paper and ribbon accents give each pocket a feel of its own while a silk flower bloom adds playfulness to the page.

Erin Smith, Phoenix, Arizona

Supplies: Patterned paper; heart clip, word concho, metal square charm (7 Gypsies); tags (Avery); hinges, mini brads (Making Memories); label maker (Dymo); fibers (Ek Success); vellum; ribbon; hemp; silk flower; ticket stub; cardstocks

These fish were in a tank in our hotel lobby when I went to Dallas in Feb. 2004 for the Hobby Industry Association (HIA) trade show. I have thought about them a lot since that weekend.

When I started scrapbooking seriously in early 2003, I never in a million years could have predicted where this hobby would lead me. It doesn't seem possible that within two years, I went from hating my pages and compulsively redoing them, to being named a 2004 Memory Makers Master, to appearing on the cover of Memory Makers Magazine, to seeing my own chapter in a book!

Until this hobby, I was never more than a big fish in a little pond with regards to my talents. But for the first time, a bigger world seems within my reach. I have already taken more risks, and accomplished so much more than I ever dreamed. And with each little success comes the confidence to reach for the next goal.

So what's next? Dare I dream of doing another book? Possibly a career shift either further into scrapbooking or into photography? I'm really not sure. But I believe that there is more in store for me. For now, I guess I will keep on swimming ... keep striving until I get in over my head. Right now, the water feels fine. March 2005

little fish

Little Fish

Until scrapbooking became part of Susan's world, she had always felt like a big fish trapped in a too-small pond. Now her new passion has introduced her to a much larger sea of opportunities brimming with a mounting list of accomplishments. Susan took this photo in a hotel lobby while attending an industry trade show for a fun reminder of how far she has come. Small mirror circles create a bubble effect across the spread. She scored the leaf details and applied diamond glaze to her title for shine.

Susan Cyrus, Broken Arrow, Oklahoma

Supplies: Patterned paper (Carolee's Creations); textured cardstock (Bazzill); mirror circles (JewelCraft); dimensional adhesive (JudiKins)

... is so incredibly unpredictable right now. My future, or even what I will be doing, where I will be living just 6 months from now is a big question. I know Eric will be finished with grad school (finally), but I have no idea where we'll be. We'll be together – that's for sure – that's one thing I can always count on. Maybe I'll go back to school. Maybe I'll take some time off for myself. Maybe I'll try to have a baby. Who knows? Crazy how unpredictable life can be – but I love where I am, where we are right now, and I wouldn't want it any other way. (journaled 11-23-04)

My Life

Susan created this page while at a crossroads in her life to help her work through the uncertainty she was experiencing and to embrace the unknown. She stamped her title on canvas patches and stitched along each for a well-worn look. Susan then stamped the word "time" on a small tag attached to velvet ribbon with a safety pin to begin her journaling passage and to enhance her photo.

Susan Weinroth, Centerville, Minnesota

Supplies: Patterned papers (Basic Grey); textured cardstock (Bazzill); foam letter stamps, rub-on words, tag, safety pin (Making Memories); letter stamps (Ma Vinci's Reliquary); photo turns (7 Gypsies); ribbon (May Arts); canvas fabric; stamping ink; brads

New Perspective

After her youngest child headed off to college, Becky was surprised to realize she could embrace this new season of her life with hopeful anticipation. Journaling written over two patterned papers reveals how after years of focusing on her children and their needs, Becky could now turn her attention to pursuing other passions. An upbeat photo and cheery colors perfectly capture the positive theme of her attitude and her layout.

Becky Novacek, Fremont, Nebraska
Photo: Vicki Chrisman, North Bend, Nebraska

Supplies: Patterned papers (Chatterbox, Scrapworks); letter stamps (FontWerks, Ma Vinci's Reliquary); letter stickers (American Crafts); ribbons (May Arts); twill (Jo-Ann Stores); photo corners (Canson); stamping ink; pen

Desert Dreams

Texture and shine make Jen's desert dreams come alive on this page that looks ahead to the next five years. Here she reveals her plans for an adobe-style house surrounded by desert beauty. Jen embossed a brick texture plate into copper foil which was then heated and inked for color. Texture paint was then added to mimic the look of stucco which perfectly complements her idyllic background papers.

Jen Lowe, Lafayette, Colorado

Supplies: Patterned paper (PSX Design); lightweight copper (AMACO); texture plate, flowers, die-cut letters, photo corners (Spellbinders); hinge; patterned vellum (EK Success); texture paint (Delta); alcohol inks (Ranger)

Aspiring Mother

Holly shares her ambitions for her legacy as a mother in this soft and dreamy page. Her journaling expresses her desire to be the best mother she can possibly be and for her children to hold fast to the values and qualities she aspires to instill in them. Ornate metal rosettes give the page a timeless strength and beauty, as do the combination of color and black-and-white photos.

Holly VanDyne, Mansfield, Ohio

Supplies: Patterned paper (Junkitz); fabric tags (Jo-Ann Stores); metal rosettes (EK Success); letter stamps (Leave Memories); date stamp (Making Memories); stamping ink; transparency

If I Live to Be 100

Life abounds on Phillipa's page, which is dedicated to the ambitions she would like to bring to fruition before she turns 100. Journaling tags tucked behind torn patterned paper elements are topped with flower buttons and lace for feminine beauty and dimension. She also chalked around the edges of the tags for softer transitions.

Phillipa Campbell, Jerrabomberra, New South Wales, Australia

Supplies: Patterned papers (Anna Griffin, Me & My Big Ideas, Patchwork Paper Design, Rusty Pickle); letter stickers (Creative Imaginations); postage frame (www.maudeandmillie.com); acrylic paint; chalk; lace; buttons; thread; fabric

Turning 30 is supposed to be hard. As I neared that milestone, I heard over and over ... "oh, no – your going to be thirty," said with pity as if I were nearing 100 instead of thirty. I was actually looking forward to thirty. It seemed as if my chronological age was catching up with my emotional age. I've always felt older than my actual age. For the first time since adolescence, I realized that I was actually feeling my age. That is a nice thing. I've experienced so much in my first 30 years – laughter, pain, fear, happiness – all of which helped me to grow into the woman that I am today. I feel as if my life has begun to settle itself into something more "grown up" which is a really wonderful place to be. Over time, I've grown from a baby to a child to a teenager to a young adult to an adult. I've taken on a variety of roles – wife, stepmother, student, and employee. All of these roles have had an impact on who I am and what I want as I enter my thirties. I'm excited about what is to come and what I may become. This page will explore some of the things that I am facing as I enter the next stage of my life.
— Amy Melniczenko, May 2004

Career. As I near completion of my MBA, I can't help but wonder what I will do with the rest of my life. I've always been very ambitious and usually I knew what path I wanted to take. Initially, I thought that social work would be a wonderful career path for me. Unfortunately, it became obvious to me, eventually, that I could not do direct service work with clients for the long-term. As I turned my attention on my desire to receive a Masters degree, business administration seemed to be a good complement to my earlier degree and work experiences. I also hoped the MBA program would help me to figure out what I wanted to be when I grew up. Unfortunately, it hasn't been quite that simple. I know that finding fulfilling, interesting work will be important for me. I need to find a career path that will be meaningful to me and give me a sense of purpose that I do not have now. I certainly have a lot of interests but I don't know how to turn those interests into a career path. That will be my next hurdle ... figuring out what I can do with my life, career-wise, that will make me happy and give me a sense of completion.

turning 30

Motherhood. As I become 30, my greatest wish is to become a mother. We have been trying for a little over a year with no luck. It has, however, been a bit elusive for us. We are exploring our options and trying to stay positive but it's been a very trying experience for me. I have had to face issues that I never anticipated experiencing in my journey towards motherhood. I have had to come to terms with the fact that I may not experience pregnancy and biological motherhood despite the fact that I've wanted it my entire life. I hope that one day I will be able to overcome the issues we'll have to face with respect to infertility but if we can't I think that I have finally worked through it to the point that I would be okay. I try not to dwell on the negative aspects of infertility. I try to focus on the fact that it has brought Paul and I closer than I could have imagined. It has truly given us the opportunity to create a more cohesive and supportive marriage. It has also allowed me to pay more attention to my body and try to understand it. This has already had a positive impact on my health. Rather than be devastated over our difficulties, I have tried to dwell on the positive things in my life. Sure, I want to be a mommy one day but I also have a great life now and I'm trying to enjoy it for what it is instead of what it isn't without a baby. The near future will include a focus on improving my health and getting our lives ready for the baby that we hope will one day join our family.

Self-Improvement. Another challenge for me in my 30s will be to work on some of the issues that I've struggled with and find a way to work them out. I'm a strong supporter of the notion that it is important to know yourself and try to continuously improve whatever you see in yourself that you'd like to change. I have a lot of insecurities and negative behavior patterns that I'd like to see altered. I have severe body image problems that affect my ability to be comfortable in my own skin. Having once felt comfortable in my body, it is difficult to no longer feel any affinity to it today. I need to find a way to be okay with my body and not focus on the unrealistic body image shown so often in the media. I need to find a way to be comfortable with me – the good, the bad and the ugly. I also need to work on a couple of behavioral issues such as my dislike of spontaneity, my need for control, and my possessiveness and control issues. I've also been told that I can occasionally be difficult because of my reliance on whining when I don't get what I want. Again, that is related to my possessiveness and control issues. I need to overcome those things. I also want to focus on cultivating in myself the qualities that I admire in other people such as kindness, focus, generosity, optimism, assertiveness, and openness to experience. I am a work in progress but I think that with awareness and hard work, I can find a way to improve myself and become the person that I want to be for the remainder of my life.

Turning 30

To keep the focus on her reflective journaling, Amy kept the design of her two-page spread understated by choosing serene colors and printing directly onto her cardstock backgrounds. Journaling blocks detail Amy's thoughts on her life journey thus far, as well as aspirations she holds near and dear to her heart as a milestone birthday approaches. The perspective of her photo and linear design of her title treatment artfully emphasize her page theme of looking forward.

Amy Melniczenko, Chesterfield, Virginia

Supplies: Patterned paper, letter stickers (KI Memories); textured cardstock (Bazzill)

Note to self

In her book, Write It Down, Make It Happen, Dr. Henriette Klauser suggests that just documenting your goals can be the first crucial step in making them a reality. "Writing it down is about clearing your head, identifying what you want, and setting your intent. You can 'make it happen' purely by believing in the possibility." Sharing your personal ambitions in your scrapbooks is an excellent way to define what you want for yourself and for your life. These pages will stand as testimony to the fact that you believe your goals can and will be achieved. "Writing down your dreams and aspirations is like hanging up a sign that says, 'Open for Business,'" notes Klauser. Moreover, documenting your dreams helps create your own personal "to-do list" in addition to establishing a sense of accountability. Once it's written down in your journaling, you can take pride in reporting your successes—complete with triumphant photos. So go ahead and scrapbook all the things you want for yourself. . .and see what happens next!

My Self

Wanting to use expressive patterned paper in a way that the phrases could still be read, Johanna mounted a torn section from a second sheet on foam adhesive spacers. She typed her journaling on a library card, communicating her satisfaction with life thus far, along with characteristics she hopes to improve upon. Johanna embellished a film negative strip with letter stickers, ribbons and a jigsaw letter for a collage-style title and used the punched-out portion as a photo accent.

Johanna Peterson, El Cajon, California
Photo: Aubrey Harns, Alpine, California

Supplies: Patterned paper (Mystic Press); chipboard letter, safety pin, ribbon, brads, paint (Making Memories); letter cut-outs (Footala); word charm (Colorbök); metal label holder (Jo-Ann Stores); ribbons (Michaels); twill ribbon (Creative Impressions); date stamp (Hero Arts); letter stickers (EK Success); mini buttons (Trims and Buttons); photo corners (3M); library pocket (Anima Designs); library card (Boxer Scrapbook Productions); wood-grain label tape (source unknown); cardstock; walnut ink; negative strip

Star Light
Star Bright

Jane's softly swirling layout glistens in honor of wishing upon stars. Journaling printed onto shimmering vellum recalls childhood wishes sent up above, as well as Jane's grown-up wishes she now hopes come true. A star stencil was used to create dynamic movement on the page, layering the purple and white vellum shapes to dance across the design in celestial celebration.

Jane Swanson, Janesville, Wisconsin

Supplies: Patterned cardstock, shimmering purple and white vellums, star stencil, metal-rimmed tag (Club Scrap); metal corner charms, metal ribbon charm (www.maudeandmillie.com); ribbon; brads

Dare to Dream

As Jennifer set out to create a page about herself, it transformed into a tribute to her dreams—those that have already come true and those that will someday. Already blessed with a family of her own, she included reminders on the page of her "happily ever after"—her marriage and her daughter she affectionately dubbed "Lainey Bug," represented in a metal ladybug plaque. Jennifer used image-editing software to combine her four self-portraits into one large photo, using a brush tool to soften the edges.

Jennifer Johner, Asquith, Saskatoon, Canada

Supplies: Patterned paper, stickers, rub-on words, canvas tags (Creative Imaginations); textured cardstock (Bazzill); rub-on words, metal label holders, brads, eyelet words, metal plaque, foam letter stamps, paint (Making Memories); metal word charm (Pebbles); letter sticker (Sweetwater); image-editing software (Adobe Photoshop); silk flowers; ribbon

Overwhelming

Cori's first house purchase came with a lot of potential...and a lot of work! She designed this page to document her home-improvement aspirations and to help her overcome the "project overload" that could immobilize her good intentions. She chose patterned paper to reflect the sense of chaos and objects-in-motion feel to match the spirit of her topic. Machine stitching on either side of the photos stabilizes the design and lends a sense of organization.

Cori Dahmen, Vancouver, Washington

Supplies: Patterned paper (Keeping Memories Alive); letter and number stickers (Doodlebug Design); ribbons (SEI); mini brads (Bazzill); transparency

I Resolve

Courtney dove into the new year by designing a page dedicated to her resolutions. She boldly stamped the words "I resolve. . ." in alternating lowercase and capital letters, listing each goal in her own handwriting. To achieve these goals as she enters her 30th year, Courtney hangs this layout in her office as a constant reminder and source of motivation.

Courtney Walsh, Winnebago, Illinois

Supplies: Patterned papers, letter stickers, rivets (Chatterbox); textured cardstock (Bazzill); letter stamps (PSX Design); stamping ink; gel pen; cheesecloth

My Passion

For as long as she can remember, Colleen has loved books. Here she features a few favorites from her collection, neatly tied up like the gift they represent in her life. Her journaling expresses her dream to someday have a published book of her own join the ranks on her bookshelf. She used aged and book-print patterned papers to convey the timeless quality of books and added leather ties and lace for classic style.

Colleen Stearns, Natrona Heights, Pennsylvania

Supplies: Patterned papers (Basic Grey, Karen Foster Design, Paper Loft, 7 Gypsies); ribbon (May Arts); tag (Rusty Pickle); decorative brads, metal-rimmed tag, photo corner (Making Memories); distress ink (Ranger); string; leather ties; lace

Dreams Change

Holly used an image of herself at age 24 to contrast with the image of the family she now embraces rather than material things she used to dream about. Her vellum-printed journaling describes the drive and determination she once had as a real estate agent to pursue a life of "bigger and better." Now Holly's drive and determination has simply been redirected—to her family. Touches of ribbon, rickrack die cuts accented with mini eyelets and embellished wooden frames help create a homespun charm and a page rich in love.

Holly Corbett, Central, South Carolina
Photo: Wal-Mart, Anderson, South Carolina

Supplies: Patterned papers (KI Memories, 7 Gypsies); textured cardstocks (Bazzill, Close To My Heart); wooden frames, word plaque (Li'l Davis Designs); die-cut letters, rickrack die cut (QuicKutz); mini eyelets (Making Memories); letter stamps (Hero Arts); calendar page; vellum; stamping ink; ribbon; silk

Goals for 2005

Documenting goals in writing helps solidify them in our minds, which is why Maria took things a step further by incorporating them into a scrapbook page. She printed each goal for the year on a separate strip of paper using a variety of fonts for playful appeal. She then accented the strips with brads, eyelets and a belt end for a unique look that complements her assortment of patterned papers.

Maria Burke, Steinbach, Manitoba, Canada
Photo: Howard Doerksen, Steinbach, Manitoba, Canada

Supplies: Patterned papers (Daisy D's, K & Company, Making Memories, Mustard Moon, Provo Craft, SEI); flower sticker (Creative Imaginations); decorative element and number stickers (Wordsworth); letter stickers (Daisy Hill); belt end (Scrapworks); photo turns (Making Memories, 7 Gypsies); eyelets, snaps, square brads (Making Memories)

I Cherish...

my most profound gifts and most simple pleasures. My home, my
hobbies, my relationships and my secret escapes. I cherish my sentimental
treasures, favorite indulgences and unabashed obsessions. Stolen moments
of solitude. Guilty, silly, unexpected sources of happiness. I cherish the
passions and interests that enrich and fulfill my life.

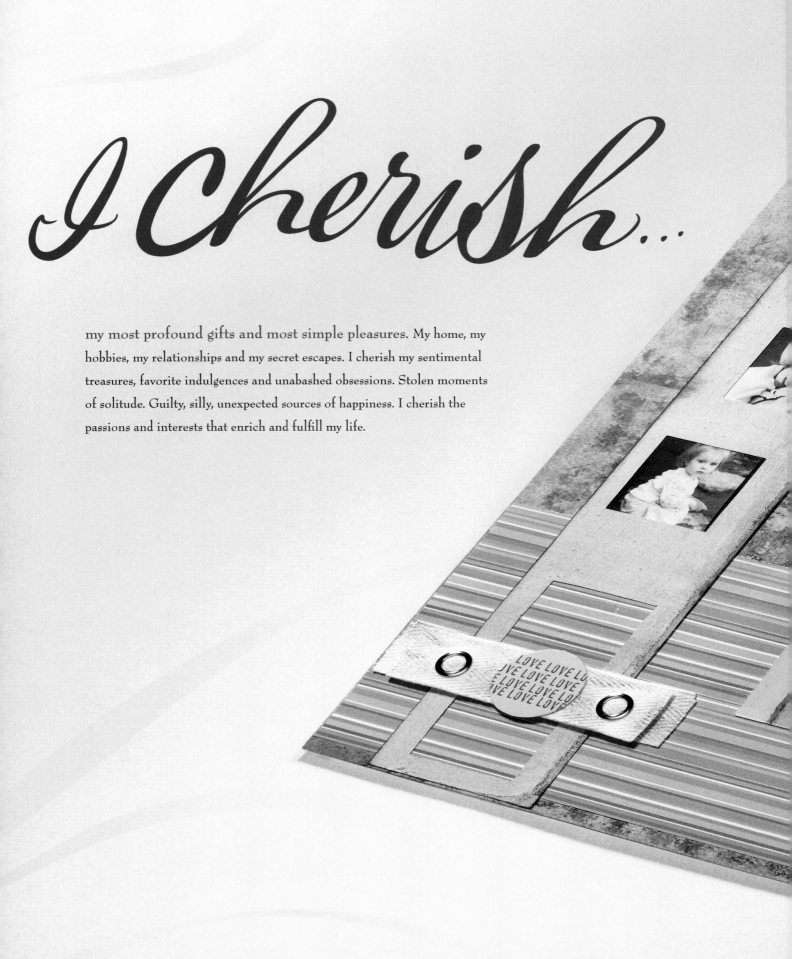

My Home On the Range

Here Becky pays tribute to the rustic beauty of Montana and the open range she calls home. To further showcase the 2,000-acre ranch that has captured her heart, she created an accordion book that houses sanded-edge photos and detail-rich journaling. Mounted to the page, the book is tied closed with strands of leather accented with aged bone beads. The striking tassel accent was created using a leather strap and horse hair secured with a conch. A page pebble highlights Becky's home on map paper while torn and chalked papers and frayed fabrics add to the layout's rustic feel.

Becky Fleck, Columbus, Montana

Supplies: Patterned papers (K & Company, Paper Loft, Pebbles, Sweetwater); textured cardstock (Bazzill); lacing cord (BraidCraft); glass beads (Mill Hill); metal label holder (Making Memories); cowhide leather, aged bone beads (Leather Factory); metal conch (source unknown); cloth plaid napkin; horse hair; eyelets; brads

I Love This Old Town

Though she only lived there for three short years, Abingdon, Virginia, is where Jane's heart will always reside. She included images of the historic town's beloved happenings, capturing the feel of a simpler time. Jane cut out images from select photos, such as that of the plaque, and elevated them with foam adhesive spacers atop other photos from around town. The inked edges and black photo corners provide finishing touches of yesteryear on a place that will forever remain special.

Jane Rife, Hendersonville, Tennessee

Supplies: Patterned paper (Karen Foster Design); photo corners (Canson); gold medallions (Blumenthal Lansing); flat-head brads (All My Memories); number stickers (Scrapworks); stamping ink; eyelets; cardstock

My Special Treasures

Deborah made a top-10 list of her favorite sentimental treasures and took a photo of the objects together for artful documentation. She numbered each to correspond with the descriptions beneath the photo as well as the reason why she loves each in the accompanying journaling passage. The photo of her treasures lifts to reveal a close-up image of those things held dear.

Deborah Conken, Riverside, California

Supplies: Patterned papers (Amscan, Anna Griffin, K & Company, 7 Gypsies); textured cardstock (Bazzill); stencil letter (Hunt Corp.); script stamp (Hero Arts); heart snaps, foam letter stamps, photo hinges, photo turns, brads (Making Memories); slide mount (Jest Charming); letter stickers (EK Success); red tacks, windows and frames (Chatterbox); copper word charm (Foofala); cork sticker numbers (Creative Imaginations); fibers (Colorbök); metal bookmark clip (Manto Fev); ribbon (Offray); distress inks (Ranger); pigment powders (Jacquard Products); acrylic paint

I Love Shoes and Bags

An affinity for all things feminine is embodied on Phillipa's shoe and handbag tribute. She showcased a photo of her favorite foot décor of the moment, as well as a bag passed down from her mother (the obsession appears to be genetic!). She staggered blocks of flowers and frills, layering different patterns of floral-print papers for a quiltlike effect. Buttons and lace add the perfect finishing touches to this ensemble, much like the subjects themselves.

Phillipa Campbell, Jerrabomberra, New South Wales, Australia

Supplies: Patterned papers (Anna Griffin); pewter letters (Making Memories); letter stickers (EK Success); letter stamps (Hero Arts); heart punch (Emagination Crafts); vellum; buttons; lace; charm; pearl pin; ribbon; thread; acrylic paint; stamping ink

Our Style

Here Jenn combined two of her favorite passions—scrapbooking and home decorating—to design this richly textured page. Photos that detail individual home décor elements as well as remnants of fabric and wallpaper create a layout that reflects Jenn's personal style and represents an outward expression of her individuality and tastes. Jenn used gold medium to alter the silver metal frame and to create her embossed title. Journaling is revealed beneath the hinged bottom photo.

Jenn Brookover, San Antonio, Texas

Supplies: Patterned papers (Daisy D's, 7 Gypsies); textured cardstock (Bazzill); mesh (Creative Imaginations); letter stamps (Ma Vinci's Reliquary); gold clips (7 Gypsies); fiber (On The Surface); handmade button (My Imaginary Room); keyhole (Li'l Davis Designs); wax finish (AMACO); staples, hinges, metal letters, frame (Making Memories); metallic rub-ons (Craf-T); acrylic paint; paint chip; fabric; wallpaper sample; stamping inks

When Troy and I first moved in together, we brought with us a hodge podge of belongings. From old desks to milk crates as bedside tables, we found uses for whatever we had. With new jobs and big school loans, we had to borrow garage sale furniture and a card table with chairs from our neighbors. The memories of the couch that moved every time we sat on it and the dresser with broken drawers, which we cursed at every morning as we tried to get ready for work still make us laugh. We loved our wild white couch with splashes of primary colors and our black "Techline" tables (our first purchases of "good" furniture). The 13" TV positioned ever so carefully on the hearth completed our look.

Two moves, four kids and a few sets of furniture later, our tastes have evolved a bit. Classic, eclectic, modern...there really is no one name to describe it. Our favorite piece is the fresco we had made by a local artist, Jayne Samuelson Wright. Bringing all of the colors and shapes together, it is the focal point of the downstairs. Amist baskets of kid stuff and Little Tykes toys, we have created a home that we love, decorated (from shoulder level up, anyway) in a style all our own.

Pictures from left to right: leg of dining room table, close up of hallway table (inside frame), bottom corner of Fresco, kitchen candle stick holder, family room drapes, close up of jewelry box

Piano Man Sam

Samuel, an aspiring songwriter, is passionate about playing the piano and writing the songs of his heart. He adhered a self-designed CD case to the page with an actual demo CD tucked inside. His paper weaving design was created by crumpling white cardstock, dipping it in liquid walnut crystals ink, ironing the sheets, then printing out each of his song titles. Samuel then cut the cardstock into strips and wove them into a design on the page. A musical stamp applied throughout the design adds a subtle finishing touch.

Samuel Cole, Stillwater, Minnesota

Supplies: Stamp (Raindrops On Roses); letter stickers (Creative Imaginations); typewriter letter stickers (All My Memories); folio closure (Colorbök); letter stamps (PSX Design); walnut crystals; stamping ink; transparency; pens; cardstock; fine grade sandpaper

Sanity by the *Cup*

The guilty pleasure of a daily latte may seem extravagant to some, but to sympathetic mothers everywhere it is a small price for sanity. Jennifer created this page to embrace her love for and addiction to a favorite gourmet coffee drink. She used latte-colored papers in coordination with Starbucks' iconic colors, leaving plenty of room to journal the history of how it all began—a toddler on a sleeping strike. A simple canvas tag creates a napkinlike effect and lends all the texture this page needs without disrupting the peace.

Jennifer Massaro,
South Plainfield, New Jersey

Supplies: Textured cardstocks (Bazzill); rub-on letters (Making Memories); vellum letter stickers (Mrs. Grossman's); canvas (Creative Imaginations)

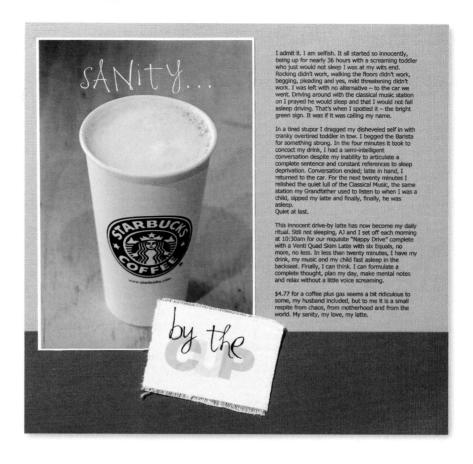

What Makes Me *Tick*

The passions of Julie's heart abound on her fun and funky design. Those things that are part of who she is are arranged in a descending order for a striking journaling element. Julie added a modern-art feel to the page by melting slides, which she painted first then layered with a clear embossing pad and covered with extra thick embossing powder. By holding a heat embossing gun up close, the slides melted into whimsical shapes.

Julie Geiger, Gold Canyon, Arizona

Supplies: Patterned paper (KI Memories); textured cardstock (Bazzill); slide mounts (Magic Scraps); letter stencil (Wordsworth); word stickers (Creative Imaginations); letter stickers (Pebbles); date stamp, mini brads (Making Memories); clock stamp (Inkadinkado); letter stamps (FontWerks); extra thick embossing powder (Suze Weinberg); acrylic paints; stamping ink; paper clips; ribbon

My Story

Sage added a functional, fold-out accordion book to pocket tags of her favorite things. With a two-page layout, she was able to encapsulate the heart of who she is through the loves that define her. Sage incorporated numerous textures and fibers into her design and stamped her own background patterns. She kept the pages simple, yet fun, with plenty of room for hand-penned journaling.

Sage Hoopiiaina for Stampin' Up!, Sandy, Utah

Supplies: Cardstocks, letter stamps, vine stamps, stamping ink, embossing powders, colored markers, tag sheets, dimensional adhesive (Stampin' Up!); watermark ink (Tsukineko); linen thread; circle punches; staples; brads; ribbon; fiber; hemp; wire

Note to self

Many people are hesitant about starting to scrapbook themselves because they don't want to start a separate project. They feel like they don't have the time to commit to working on a separate album based solely upon their lives. So why not include pages about yourself in your family albums? When you scrapbook pages for your family albums, you likely include all sorts of different topics related to family life. You may scrap a page about your son's soccer trophy, your daughter's spelling bee win, or your husband's grilling exper-

tise. You may even create a page dedicated to the antics of the family dog. All those pages focus on featuring a single personality within the family unit. Therefore it makes perfect sense to include pages on yourself in your family album, as you are a member of your family too! Your personality and individual stories represent a crucial component of your family and help to paint a more complete picture of your life together. Be sure to incorporate pages about yourself as you chronicle the life and times of your family.

Self-Indulgence

As a self-admitted chocoholic, Nic brought out the strength of her greatest weakness in this visually rich design. A chocolate a day is a must for Nic, and she layered close-up images of her favorite treats, as well as a black-and-white photo of herself in sheer bliss. To create her title, Nic first used letter stamps for "indulgence," then applied the same word on top with a rub-on word. For "self," she applied a dimensional coating to letter stickers for shine.

Nic Howard, Pukekone,
South Auckland, New Zealand

Supplies: Patterned paper (Karen Foster Design); textured cardstocks (Bazzill); letter stamps (Ma Vinci's Reliquary); rub-on word (Making Memories); dimensional paint (Plaid); walnut ink; acrylic paint

Things I *Love*

Unimpressed by lavish handbags and ridiculously trendy fashion favorites of celebrities, Tamara came up with her own best picks on this page. Her personalized "T List" combines all things cool and great in Tamara's world. She created her own patterned paper by brushing a wash of acrylic paint and a translucent glaze over art paper which was then stamped with a decorative stencil.

Tamara Morrison, Trabuco Canyon, California

Supplies: Artist paper (Strathmore); textured cardstock (Bazzill); letter stencil (Hunt Corp.); die-cut letters (QuicKutz); foam letter stamps, rub-on letters (Making Memories); word bead (Magnetic Poetry); heart embellishment (Little Black Dress Designs); ribbon (Offray); fibers (EK Success, Funky Fibers); translucent glaze (Delta); label maker (Dymo); acrylic paint; stamping ink

Me

Rather than journal about the loves of her life, Danielle listed the passions she cherishes on small clips of paper and incorporated them throughout the page. She added elements of herself to the lay-out as well, illustrating her list of favor-ites with everything from vintage earrings to travel ephemera and Asian accents. Danielle used image-editing software to accentuate her "then" and "now" portraits, darkening the area around her current photo to highlight her face.

Danielle Thompson, Tucker, Georgia

Supplies: Patterned paper (Basic Grey); ribbon (Offray); appliques (Wrights); memorabilia pocket (Pebbles); acrylic mirror anchors (Home Depot); flower die cut (Colorbök); beaded flower (Xyron); window mounts (Deluxe Designs); vintage image (Foofala); Hawaiian image (Chronicle Books); image-editing software (Adobe Photoshop); Asian image (from an Oriental candies box); yellow and orange bead accent (found at the flea market); cardstock; beads; mini clothespins; sewing pins; airplane, Eiffel tower and camera charms; hoop earring; metal-rimmed glass charm; staples; U.S. postage stamp

Hobby or Obsession?

A photo of Julie designing her own page was the perfect way to celebrate her pas-sion for scrapbooking. Her journaling gives the history of when her obsession first began, and brilliant paper tags tied together with ribbons spell out her love for color. Julie filled her page with happy-colored bows in whimsical prints and applied extra thick embossing powder to select ephemera for a shine. The numbers 24/7 were added to demonstrate just how serious this "hobby" has become.

Julie Johnson, Seabrook, Texas

Supplies: Patterned paper (KI Memories); textured cardstock, chipboard circles (Bazzill); chipboard letters (Li'l Davis Designs); letter stickers (American Crafts, Creative Imaginations, Wordsworth); colored brads (Making Memories); punches (EK Success, McGill); extra thick embossing powder (Ranger); chalk ink (Clearsnap); ribbons; pinking shears

My Greatest *Love*

A newfound passion for paper prompted Rachel to create this colorful page dedicated to her obsession. In her defense, Rachel insists her love affair is but a means to an end for scrapbooking her family memories. She color-blocked her background and used a square punch to create an eye-appealing paper grid element. Rachel created a frame for her letter-pebble word by cutting a square from the center of a photo featuring part of her paper collection.

Rachel Ludwig, Abbotsford,
British Columbia, Canada

Supplies: Patterned papers (Carolee's Creations, KI Memories, Magenta, PSX Design); textured cardstocks (Bazzill, DMD); letter stamps (PSX Design); rub-on letters (Making Memories); letter pebbles (Li'l Davis Designs); photo corners (Canson); stamping ink; thread

In Love With *Color*

Polly's cheerful salute to color commands the eye with vibrant paint chips and patterned papers. She cleverly combined accents such as decorative buttons, bows, tickets and silk flowers with coordinating paint chips for dimension and flare. Polly's die-cut-accented photo and journaling tag enhance as well as personalize the page.

Polly McMillan, Bullhead City, Arizona

Supplies: Patterned papers (Chatterbox, Paper Fever); ribbon (Offray); letter stamps (FontWerks, PSX Design); bottle cap (Li'l Davis Designs); raffle tickets (www.maudeandmillie.com); letter stickers (Creative Imaginations) decorative buttons (Blumenthal Lansing, Junkitz); heart punch (EK Success); die-cut letters (QuicKutz); buttons; rickrack; silk flowers

Extra *Value'd*

Melanie finds her happy place under the golden arches, where with the magic of McDonald's fries, a cheeseburger and a fountain drink, suddenly all is well. She chose the restaurant's trademark colors for her background and cleverly overlaid them with actual sandwich wrappers stitched into place. Melanie stamped words she wanted to highlight in her journaling and included a photo of the restaurant sign wrapped like a gift.

Melanie Bauer, Columbia, Missouri
Photo: Andrew Bauer, Columbia, Missouri

Supplies: Patterned paper (Chatterbox); textured cardstocks (Bazzill); ribbon, hinges (Making Memories); letter stamps (PSX Design); pen; stamping ink; McDonald's sandwich wrappers

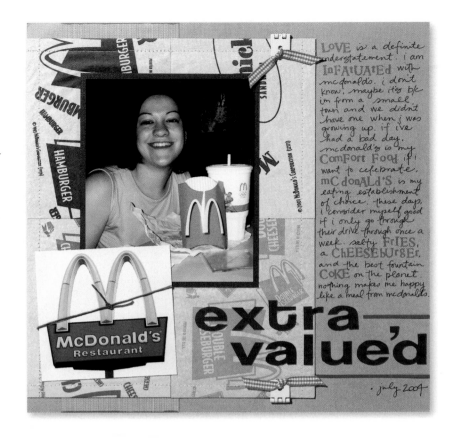

*T*ime

To Renee, the most valuable gift anyone can give her is an unbroken interval of time alone. For as much as she loves her family, time to rejuvenate her soul with a quiet block of time all her own is what it takes for her to give the best of herself. The large close-up photo of the clock lifts on hinges to share her love for her family and for precious time to refresh and regroup. The bottom of the page is accented with images of the activities she embraces in her solitude which include crafting, reading and surfing the Internet.

Renee Foss, Seven Fields, Pennsylvania

Supplies: Patterned papers, hinges, clock charm (K & Company); textured cardstock (Bazzill); foam letter stamps, rub-on letters, epoxy stickers (Making Memories); file tab (7 Gypsies); clock hands (Jest Charming); watermark ink (Tsukineko); eyelets; brads; ribbon

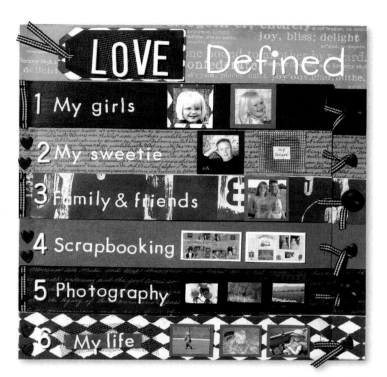

Love Defined

Since one page was not enough to encompass all the joys of Sue's life, she doubled her space with numbered, flip-style strips. Each lifts by a ribbon pull to reveal miniature images, playful accents and journaling printed on vellum that describes her appreciation for each blessing. Her girls, husband, family and friends are all celebrated on this heartfelt tribute which also includes Sue's love of scrapbooking, photography and her life as a whole.

Sue Travassos, Rosedale, British Columbia, Canada

Supplies: Patterned papers (7 Gypsies, Rusty Pickle); textured cardstock (Bazzill); letter stickers (Memories Complete); rub-on letters, brads (Making Memories); ribbon (Offray); buttons (source unknown); plastic letters and numbers (Staples); heart brads (Creative Impressions); stamping ink

Kid Flick Junkie

As a movie buff, Christine created this page to highlight her favorite films—children's movies! Her self-professed passion for kid flicks stems from their refreshingly "optimistic, every-thing-always-turns-out-OK, happy feeling." Christine's cheerful page boasts an accordion booklet listing all the movies she's seen in the past six years along with her personal rating for each. Also included are ticket stubs tucked into the booklet's cover pocket which is adorned with packing tape transfer images.

Christine Brown, Hanover, Minnesota

Supplies: Textured cardstock (Bazzill); chipboard letters (Li'l Davis Designs); letter stickers (Creative Imaginations); metal-rimmed tag (Making Memories); manila tag (American Tag Co.); ribbon (Michaels); eyelets; transparency; filmstrip; preservatives; movie box images; packing tape

I achieve...

contentment in my own skin. Self-worth, self-love and pride in my one-of-a-kind successes. I achieve victories over my insecurities and triumphs over my obstacles. I accomplish milestones daily in the raising of my children. In the home and family I have established. In the optimism and strength I hold firm to when tested. I achieve emotional, physical, attitudinal and professional feats.

...I DID NOT WANT TO BE STRAPPED TO A
...SPITAL BED WEARING AN UGLY BLUE GOWN.
...NOT WANT NEEDLES AND IVS AND TUBES PROTRUDING FROM ME
...NOT WANT BRISK WALKING NURSES IN
...SCRUBS WIELDING GLOVED HANDS NEAR ME
...T TO BE TOLD WHAT TO DO OR WHEN TO DO IT.

...OT WANT TO BE NUMB.

... BODY - MY CHILD'S - EVERY MOVE.
...STAND - TO SIT - IF I CHOSE TO.
...OR IN MY BATHTUB.
...N TO SOFT MUSIC.
...THE GLOW OF CANDLELIGHT.
...HIS STRENGTH BESIDE ME
...IRTH SONG.
...SURROUNDED
...T TO ME.
...THE
...TH.

HOME BIRTH

...ild is born

December 28th 2002

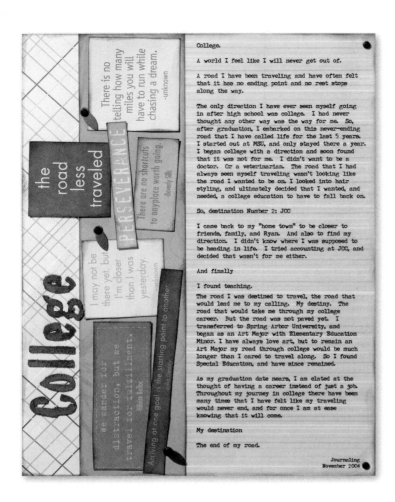

College

Nicole's page tells the story of the road she traveled while chasing a dream. . .she just wasn't certain of what the dream looked like. She explored several career options after high school, all of which left her seeking more. Finally at peace and ready to soar, Nicole has discovered her calling to teach special education. She used the bulk of her page to trace her career journey and filled the other portion with a collage of corresponding quotes accented with photo turns.

Nicole Barczak, Jackson, Michigan

Supplies: Patterned paper (KI Memories); iron-on letters (SEI); photo turns (Making Memories); brads; stamping ink

Sensible Shoes

The real Erika stands up and takes a bow of recognition in her layout dedicated to authenticity and favoring practicality over fashion. Her journaling expresses her journey of trading in blond hair for the beauty of her natural color and rejecting the control of the ever-present fashion police. Erika celebrates the arrival of becoming comfortable in her own skin by using earthy tones of nature and simplistic patterns.

Erika Follansbee, Goffstown, New Hampshire
Photo: David Follansbee, Goffstown, New Hampshire

Supplies: Patterned paper, die cuts (KI Memories); letter stickers (SEI, Sticker Studio); definition (Making Memories)

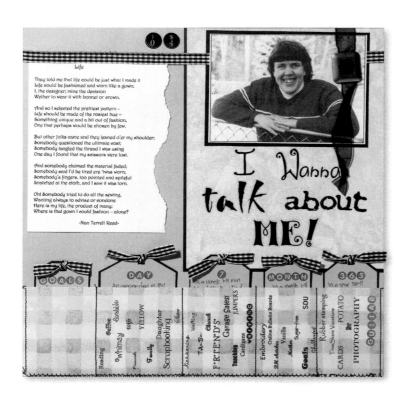

I Wanna Talk About Me!

Sharyn stepped outside her scrapbooking box to reflect on herself for a moment. She stitched pockets onto the bottom of the page for housing individual journaling tags. Each pocket shares something different including the goals she would like to achieve in the future as well as those she accomplishes in an average day, week, month and year. Sharyn printed words representative of each category directly onto her patterned paper using a variety of fonts for added fun.

Sharyn Tormanen, Howell, Michigan
Photo: Julie Laakso, Howell, Michigan

Supplies: Patterned papers (Daisy D's, Scrap Ease); textured cardstock (Bazzill); letter stickers (Creative Imaginations, Provo Craft, Wordsworth); number stickers (EK Success); ribbon (Close To My Heart); metal ribbon charm (Making Memories); cardstock; stamping ink

My Life's Work

Festive colors and patterns cheer the successes in life that Torrey holds dear to her heart. She designed this dimensional page by cutting windows into foam core board to create a series of shadow boxes to house transparency-printed images. Each window highlights a different aspect of Torrey's "life's work," which is defined in detail on an attached journaling page. By lifting up the foam core connected by hinges, Torrey reveals her triumphs in each respective window.

Torrey Scott, Thornton, Colorado
Photo: Kelli Noto, Centennial, Colorado

Supplies: Patterned papers (All My Memories, Bo-Bunny Press); embossed vellum (source unknown); ribbons (Michaels, Offray); letter stencils (U.S. Stamp & Sign Co.); hinges, rub-on letters (Making Memories); acrylic buckle (Junkitz); chalk ink (Clearsnap); cardstock; foam core board; embroidery floss; acrylic paint; transparency; buttons

I Am *Happy* to Be Me

Proud of her many achievements in life at a young age, Alecia used this page to celebrate those accomplishments and count her many blessings. Various patterned papers treated with ink provide visual appeal while passage and strip-style journaling elements detail Alecia's good fortune. She created the small home accent with cardstock and patterned paper and added crystal lacquer to the letters for shine, then enhanced photos of her children with paint.

Alecia Ackerman Grimm, Atlanta, Georgia
Photo: Deborah Ackerman,
Alpharetta, Georgia

Supplies: Patterned paper (Daisy D's, K & Company, Li'l Davis Designs, 7 Gypsies); textured cardstock (SEI); mini tags (Making Memories); scrappers block (PM Designs); label maker (Dymo); ribbon (Bobbin); buttons (Junkitz); distress ink (Ranger); plastic slide mounts; crayon; acrylic paint

Finally *Happy* With Me

Tricia's page reflects her sheer joy to finally "be among the happy," after years of battling depression. She created this page as a collage of meaningful ephemera. Bright colors and playful textures celebrate the strength Tricia employed to arrive at her "happy place" in life and the joy she finds now in helping others to do the same.

Tricia Rubens, Castle Rock, Colorado

Supplies: Patterned papers (Li'l Davis Designs, Rusty Pickle); printed transparency; key (K & Company); rub-on letters, chipboard letters (Rusty Pickle); stickers (Li'l Davis Designs, Me & My Big Ideas, Paper Loft); leather flowers, decorative brad (Making Memories); metal photo turns (7 Gypsies); metal word plaque (EK Success); paper clip; buttons; mini playing card; stencil; ticket stubs; game spinner; ribbon; stamping ink; tag

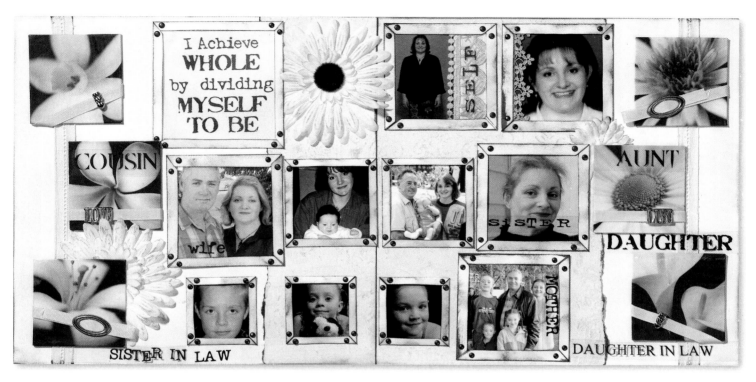

I *Achieve* Whole By Dividing Myself to Be...

Colleen achieves her sense of identity through a combination of several unique roles. Here she celebrates each with a collection of images housed inside mitered frames that have been treated with brown ink and accented with brads. Colleen extended the gallery by cutting black-and-white flowers from patterned paper, adhering them to mat squares with spray adhesive and brayering each. After the corners were trimmed and secured, each block was then coated with a glossy medium.

Colleen Macdonald, Winthrop, Australia

Supplies: Patterned papers (K & Company. Stamp It); cotton ribbon (EK Success); mat squares (Magenta); buckles (7 Gypsies); metal words. clasps (Beads & Plenty More); mini brads (Lasting Impressions); glossy medium (Ranger); cardstock; ribbon; transparencies; silk flowers; lace; stamping ink

The Pages of My Life

Wanting to simplify the process for her children to trace her life story, Christine amassed the major milestones and achievements of her life into a single easy-to-follow layout. An abbreviated autobiography of her life thus far is housed in a booklet with pages relating to her home/family, education/career and life events/hobbies. To illustrate how each of these areas overlap, the top portion of each page is comprised of an acetate timeline. When the individual timelines are overlaid, the viewer can see a complete overview.

Christine Brown, Hanover, Minnesota

Supplies: Patterned paper (Colors By Design); dragonfly stickers, pewter flower accent (Magenta); letter stamps (PSX Design); decorative photo corners (Making Memories); handmade paper (source unknown); acetate (www.pocketsonaroll.com); embossing powder; vellum; cardstocks; chalk; stamping ink

I Can Do the Splits

Barb had a million reasons why she thought she shouldn't sign up for tae kwon do, but in the spirit of health and wellness she overcame her hesitation—and found an activity she loves. Her journaling bursts with the excitement of being able to do the splits after just six weeks of training—a feat she wasn't able to accomplish as a high school cheerleader! She furthered the joyful feel with a vibrant multifont title treatment and ribbon accents that play up the image of tae kwon do belts.

Barb Hogan, Cincinnati, Ohio

Supplies: Patterned paper, rub-on letters, letter stickers (Imagination Project); textured cardstock (Bazzill); paper flower, tags (Making Memories); ribbons (Li'l Davis Designs, May Arts, Michaels); letter stamps (Stamp Craft); brad; buttons; stamping ink

Inside the layout image:

Seeing Life

Through

Wiser Eyes

There is a God.
Unconditional Love
All life is Precious
Patience will come with Practice
Choose Your Battles
You *can* do without Sleep
Kids grow up way too fast
There is no Greater Joy
Don't Sweat the Small Stuff
Pay Attention
Be There
Love is Spelled T-I-M-E
Treasure Moments
Housework will Wait
Count to Ten
We all need Limits
Nobody's Perfect, forgive yourself
Trust in God and
Smile, Laugh and Have Fun!

Of all the lessons I have learned, the most valuable have been the ones I have learned by being a mother. It is the greatest honor and privilege I have known. It is also the most difficult and exhausting experience I have ever had. Through this experience I have come to know that not only is there a God, but that he loves and cares for me and my family. I was an unbeliever until I had my first child. This was the first step of many in learning lessons that have carried me through difficult times. I never knew how strong I could be, nor did I realize the power of a Mother's love. Being patient, mostly with myself was particularly difficult. I wanted perfection from myself as a parent. Forgiving myself and moving on was a major accomplishment, and it has set me free. Doing all I had the power to do and then trusting God for the rest was not easy. Now that my children are adults, my journey as their Mother has taken a new turn. I feel their love and respect has helped to mold me into a more confident person. It is this person who will now welcome future Grandchildren into the world.

In Celebration of the Achievement of Lessons
Learned through Motherhood

Seeing *Life* Through Wiser Eyes

With children now grown, Andrea celebrates the lessons learned through the awesome adventure of motherhood on this two-page design. The left page features a portrait from a place where she can stand back and appreciate the learning experience and features a list of her acquired wisdom. The right page incorporates images from the front lines of parenthood and shares the details of the lessons that have shaped her into the woman she is today.

Andrea Lyn Vetten-Marley, Aurora, Colorado
Portrait Photo: Kelli Noto, Centennial, Colorado

Supplies: Patterned paper (Crafter's Workshop); double-sided cardstock (Creative Imaginations); decorative brads, chipboard letters (Making Memories); vellum; thread; embroidery floss; chalk ink; silk flowers

---

Note to self

A scrapbook is the perfect place to chart your progress toward specific goals. It becomes a testimony to your interests, your struggles, your hard work and, ultimately, your accomplishments. Here are some ideas for "Victory Scrapbook" layouts:

• Brainstorm all the things you would like to do, try, learn or improve about yourself and your life and include that list on a layout.

• Choose specific goals and research the steps you need to take to achieve them. Include brochures, Internet printouts and any other information. Gather them in a pocket and include them on a page.

• Journal about what you found hardest about achieving your goals and how you pressed on.

• Document the entire process of working toward your goal.

• Take "before" and "after" pictures, if applicable, as well as at various points along the way.

• Journal the feelings experienced after achieving your goal. How has your life changed?

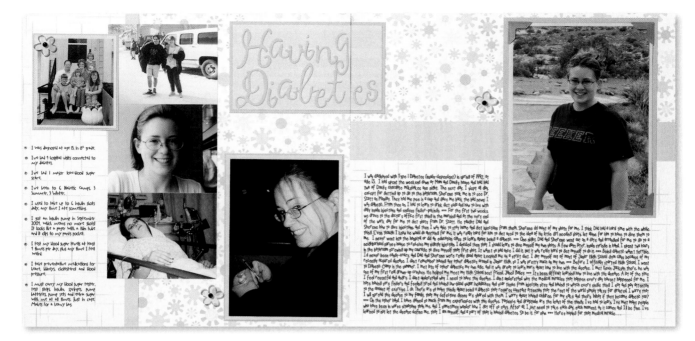

Having Diabetes

Heidi shares her journey of living with diabetes on this insightful and upbeat layout. The left page features photos of Heidi at various stages in life and also includes the major events associated with her condition in a bulleted list. The right page showcases a triumphant Heidi with journaling that gives the details of her coming to terms with diabetes and her hopes for the future.

Heidi Dillon, Salt Lake City, Utah

Supplies: Patterned paper (SEI); textured cardstock (Prism Papers); die-cut letters (Sizzix); mini eyelets (Making Memories); acrylic flowers (KI Memories); mini brads (Club Scrap); photo corners (Gary M. Burlin & Co.); stamping ink

Self

For Shannon, age not only brings wisdom but acceptance of who she is both inside and out. She used a happy and playful image of herself as the focus of the page, reflecting her being comfortable in her own skin. She added further fun and a train-track effect by creating a border of different-sized ribbons accented by brads. Shannon repeated the ribbon effect at the bottom as well, establishing a frame for her accent photo.

Shannon Taylor, Bristol, Tennessee
Photo: Robert Taylor, Bristol, Tennessee

Supllies: Patterned papers (Rusty Pickle); ribbons (American Crafts, Rusty Pickle, SEI); metal icebox tag (Karen Foster Design); mini brads (Doodlebug Design); ribbon letter charms (Making Memories); letter stickers (K & Company, Me & My Big Ideas); rub-on letters (Junkitz); dimensional adhesive (JudiKins); acrylic paint; chalk

With age comes wisdom and acceptance. I wish with all my heart I would have been accepting of myself when I was young. I was always doubting if I lived up to others expectations. Now that I'm 35, I've learned that I am okay just as I am. I like me! Sure I may not be that super-thin model of a woman but I'm not ugly. I may have an extra 20 to 25 pounds, but that doesn't make me a bad person. On occasion I get a recurrence of those old insecurities when others make a somewhat derogatory comment about my physical appearance. But you know what, I do NOT have to change myself to suit others. And if I want to change my body, I will do it for myself and no one else. And I believe that those who feel thinness is above & beyond any other human trait needs to gain a better perspective. Accept me for the person I am inside & out. I am happy with who I am.

Freedom

The decision to commit to a healthier lifestyle is embodied in the shoes Courtney showcases in this layout. Her page celebrates the freedom from her former fears and insecurities she now experiences as a faithful exerciser and focuses on what a lot of hard work, sweat and determination can do. A pullout element keeps the look of the page minimalistic, and cheerful colors help convey Courtney's carefree new attitude.

Courtney Walsh, Winnebago, Illinois

Supplies: Patterned paper (Chatterbox); textured cardstock (Bazzill, Chatterbox); ribbon (May Arts); rub-on word (Making Memories); stamping ink; gel pen

Picture Perfect

The birth of a daughter gave new life to Jennifer as well, motivating her to fully accept herself so as to instill unwavering self-love and confidence in her little girl. She created this page as a tribute to her achievement of being able to see the world, herself included, through fresh eyes. Flower accents and patterns in pretty pinks and purples exude feminine beauty. The large circle surrounding the photograph gives the illusion of a camera lens and is repeated in the use of metal-rimmed tags.

**Jennifer Bourgeault,
Macomb Township, Michigan**

Supplies: Patterned papers (Basic Grey, Chatterbox); circle cutter (Provo Craft); flower photographic stickers (Pebbles); button letters (Junkitz); purple wooden letters (Westrim); metal-rimmed tags (Making Memories); flower buttons (Doodlebug Design)

At Least I Have Good Hair

Self-confidence and self-acceptance were the inspiration for Jocelyn's stylish page. She listed the traits that she likes about her appearance and personality on the outside of her journaling envelope. Tucked inside are inked tags accented with ribbon that detail her struggles with perfection and the hope of finding balance. Layered circles, polka-dot prints and an eye-appealing combination of black and pink add bubbly energy to her design.

Jocelyn Ou, Naperville, Illinois

Supplies: Patterned paper (Autumn Leaves); textured cardstock (Bazzill, Neenah Paper); ribbon (Offray); rub-on letters (Making Memories); square brad (Scrapworks); angel charm (A Charming Place); corner rounder; stamping ink; staples; jump rings

Time for a Change

Courtney created this page for an album dedicated exclusively to improving her physical fitness. Her hidden pullout journaling focuses on her motivation for losing weight—to return to her authentic self for the sake of her family and to feel her best in her own skin. Though she has since lost the weight, the inspirational tone of her page continues to help her keep up with her goals and evokes joy in acknowledging her accomplishments.

Courtney Walsh, Winnebago, Illinois
Photo: Cindy Fassler, Dixon, Illinois

Supplies: Patterned papers (Anna Griffin, Daisy D's, Memories in the Making); metal letter charms (DieCuts with a View); ribbon (Offray); metal letters; ribbon charms; metal brad; flower brads (Making Memories); mesh (Magic Mesh); rub-on numbers (Autumn Leaves); letter stamps (PSX Design); flower accent (Hobby Lobby); gel pen; stamping ink

It's amazing how the mind plays tricks on you. It convinces you to believe in a reality that is anything but real – and because you need in your heart to cling to that belief, you accept it with open arms. In high school, my mind convinced me that I was fat – there was no such thing as "too skinny." Having been an overweigh pre-teen, it wasn't hard to see those excess pounds in spite of my relatively thin body. Weeks of not eating turned into months – and then into years... Seven altogether. Now my mind convinces me of the opposite – excess baby weight piled on like salt poured over a bowl of popcorn. But I started to believe it was okay – that I was really "me" in this body.

But photographs never lie.

This one opened my eyes and brought to mind what I already knew to be true.

It's time for a change.

It's not that I hate myself or even hate this body that brought me two beautiful children. It's that in this body, the "me" I know is gone. I'm short-tempered, quick to anger, depressed, moody, unmotivated and lethargic. Can your self image really do that to you? Yes... I think it can and it has. The old Courtney is nowhere to be found. I once read that people who doodle their name have low self esteem. For awhile, I stopped doodling my name... even though in high school it was all over my notebooks. I recently realized I've started doing it again. No one's told me I look terrible. No one's said I'll die if I don't lose weight. But I know both are true, and I need to make a change. Not just for me but for my family – for my marriage. How can you love someone else if you don't love yourself? I want my family to know the real me, and I want to experience my kids to the fullest.

So, here's to change... long overdue.

Been There *Done That*

At 35, Ramona paused to reflect on her accomplishments thus far as well as to imagine the experiences the next 35 years holds. She added creative flair to her two-part title with a ribbon-adorned letter stencil and rub-on letters for the first portion, and a combination of canvas letters, rub-on letters and stickers for the second. Ramona listed the highlights of things she can check off her "list of things to do" on a pullout card housed inside a library pocket.

Ramona Greenspan, Yorktown Heights, New York

Supplies: Patterned paper (7 Gypsies); textured cardstock (Bazzill); stencil letter, initial tab (Autumn Leaves); canvas letters, library pocket, wooden flower (Li'l Davis Designs); rub-on letters (Making Memories); stickers (K & Company); ribbon (Anna Griffin, May Arts, www.memoriesoftherabbit.com); cardstock; stamping ink; acrylic paint; staples

Snippets of My *Success*

Pamela believes in loving what you do and loves the fact that she can get paid for pursuing her passions. Since two of Pamela's three part-time jobs are centered around the use of scissors, she included shiny scissor charms on the larger mats for symbolic whimsy. The little paper scraps that form a border about the page represent "snippets"—the leftovers from her work in tailoring and scrapbooking. Pamela used larger snippets as labels for her photos that explain her fun and varied career.

Pamela James,
Ventura, California
Photos: Thom James,
Ventura, California

Supplies: Patterned paper (Creative Imaginations); textured cardstock (Bazzill); scissor charms (Blumenthal Lansing); snaps (Making Memories); embroidery floss

Journaling

I am not the type of person to sit in one place very long. Nor am I satisfied doing the same task day in and day out. It has been such an adventure creating my own career by using my passions and interests as my "job". I learned to sew as a very young girl, and by the time I was 11 years old, I made all my clothes. Later, I created one-of-a-kind outfits for all three kids. Necessity became the mother of my "first career". After the stock market crash of 1989, we found ourselves needing a second income. I let a few people know that I was planning on doing tailoring. It only took a few weeks for my calendar to fill, and now 15 years later, I am still tailoring on a nearly full-time basis.

After the birth of my second child, I felt a great desire to help women discover that childbirth can be a wonderful and exciting experience. Two years of training to become a Childbirth Educator prepared me to instruct classes in Prepared Childbirth. I have taught classes at home, at a local Birth Center and now I teach at AMGEN Pharmaceuticals in their Health and Fitness department. I have probably taught about 1000 couples techniques for a happy, healthy and less painful birth over the last 20 years.

Two years ago I began doing some freelance artwork for Memory Makers Magazine and Books. It has been such a dream come true to finally become an artist! I have been a passionate scrapbooker for about 8 years now I have had a lot of layouts published since 2001; it's such fun to see my stuff in print. Just this year, 2005, I began designing for Wishblade Personal Cutter, a computer interfaced cutting device. I can't wait to see where this opportunity leads.

I Contribute...

to my family in the role of parent, teacher and administrator of day-to-day life. To the one I love as partner and friend. I contribute my skills and knowledge as a working professional and my talents and imagination as an artist. I contribute my time and creativity to the keeping of memories. My efforts and enthusiasm to the challenges I undertake. I contribute my special gifts as pieces of myself.

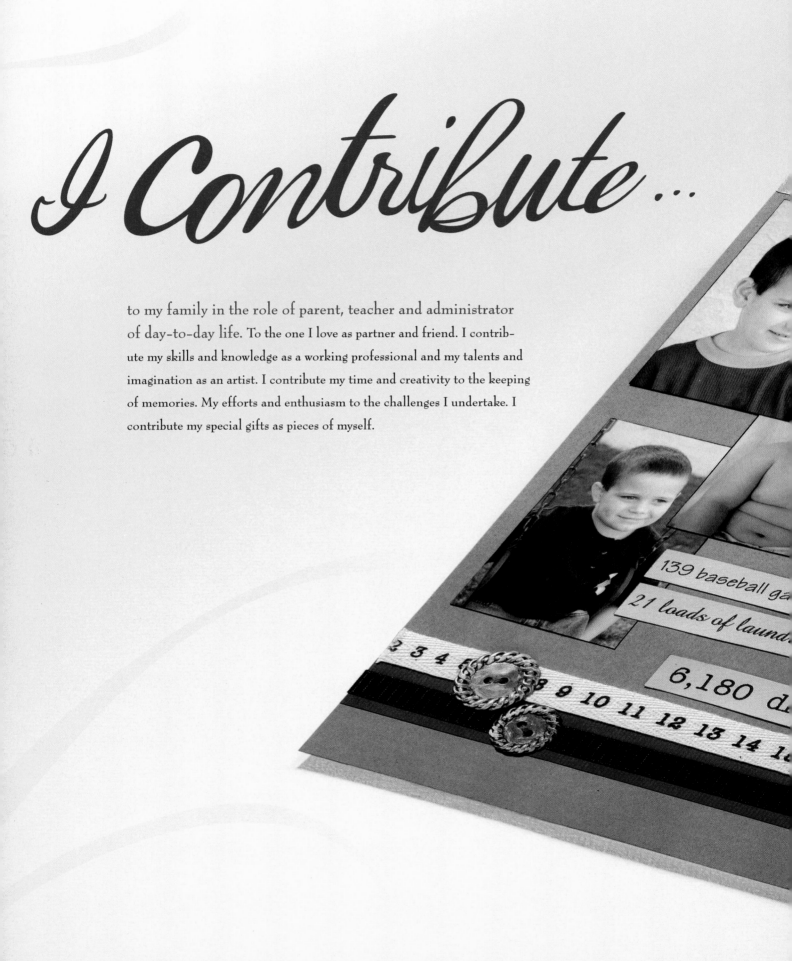

139 baseball ga

21 loads of laundr

6,180 d

RUSH!
FREE ISSUE REQUEST!

BUSINESS REPLY MAIL
FIRST-CLASS MAIL   PERMIT NO. 347   FLAGLER BEACH FL

POSTAGE WILL BE PAID BY ADDRESSEE

MEMORY
M A K E R S
PO BOX 421400
PALM COAST FL   32142-7160

SAHM

Maria created a personal tribute to her love for the best job in the world—being a stay-at-home mom. She wanted her children to always know how much she loves spending time with them and caring for them, which is captured in her journaling. Maria layered strips of colorful patterned papers accented with stapled ribbons to communicate her joy and passion for her role. She arranged metal words as a play on the popular credit card commercial to express how her job is "priceless."

Maria Burke, Steinbach, Manitoba, Canada

Supplies: Patterned papers (Anna Griffin, Daisy D's, KI Memories, Li'l Davis Designs, Rusty Pickle); letter stickers (Pebbles); metal words (Making Memories); ribbon (May Arts); metal label holder (7 Gypsies); brads

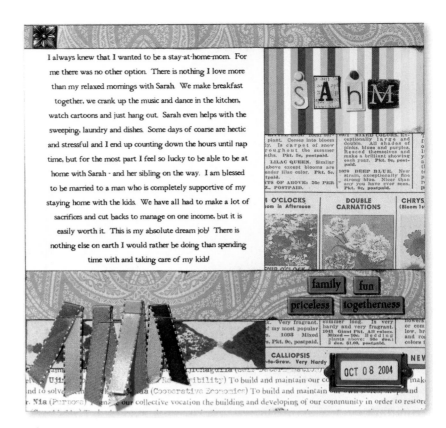

I always knew that I wanted to be a stay-at-home-mom. For me there was no other option. There is nothing I love more than my relaxed mornings with Sarah. We make breakfast together, we crank up the music and dance in the kitchen, watch cartoons and just hang out. Sarah even helps with the sweeping, laundry and dishes. Some days of coarse are hectic and stressful and I end up counting down the hours until nap time, but for the most part I feel so lucky to be able to be at home with Sarah - and her sibling on the way. I am blessed to be married to a man who is completely supportive of my staying home with the kids. We have all had to make a lot of sacrifices and cut backs to manage on one income, but it is easily worth it. This is my absolute dream job! There is nothing else on earth I would rather be doing than spending time with and taking care of my kids!

I Am Called

When faced with the question "Why do you do whatever it is that you do?" Stephanie got to work designing this tribute to being a stay-at-home wife and mother. Warm colors, patterns and accents provide a familiar and nurturing feel perfectly coupled with Stephanie's tender and reflective journaling, which is concealed beneath her hinged black-and-white portrait. She describes her love for the honor of parenting and takes a look at her world through the eyes of her heart.

Stephanie Allbaugh, Appleton, Wisconsin
Photo: Carol McCracken, Hamilton, Michigan

Supplies: Patterned papers (Anna Griffin, Paper Studio); letter stamps (EK Success, Hero Arts, Ma Vinci's Reliquary, PSX Design); metal word accent (Jo-Ann Stores); photo hinges (Making Memories); ribbon (Offray); solvent ink (Tsukineko); transparency; acrylic paint; walnut ink

Before I was a Mom
I made and ate hot meals.
I had unstained clothing.
I had quiet conversations on the phone.
Before I was a Mom
I slept as late as I wanted
And never worried about how late I got into bed.
I brushed my hair and my teeth everyday.
Before I was a Mom
I cleaned my house each day.
I never tripped over toys or forgot words to lullabies.
Before I was a Mom
I didn't worry whether or not my plants were poisonous.
I never thought about immunizations.
Before I was a Mom
I had never been puked on
Pooped on
Spit on
Chewed on
Peed on
Or pinched by tiny fingers
Before I was a Mom
I had complete control of my mind
My thoughts
My body
And my mind.
I slept all night.
Before I was a Mom
I never held down a screaming child
So that doctors could do tests
Or give shots.
I never looked into teary eyes and cried.
I never got gloriously happy over a simple grin.
I never sat up late hours at night watching a baby
sleep.
Before I was a Mom
I never held a sleeping baby just because
I didn't want to put it down.
I never felt my heart break into a million pieces
When I couldn't stop the hurt.
I never knew that something so small
Could affect my life so much.
I never knew that I could love someone so much.
I never knew I would love being a Mom.
Before I was a Mom
I didn't know the feeling of having my heart outside my
body.
I didn't know how special it could feel to feed a hungry
baby.
I didn't know that bond between a Mother and her child.
I didn't know that something so small
Could make me feel so important.
Before I was a Mom
I had never gotten up in the middle of the night
Every 10 minutes to make sure all was okay
I had never known the warmth
The joy
The love
The heartache
The wonderful moments
Or the satisfaction of being a Mom.
I didn't know I was capable of feeling so much
before I was a Mom.

Before I Was a Mom

Since Kim is rarely in any of her own photos, she wanted to create a layout for this one taken when her first child was just 3 months old. The poem proved to be a perfect fit to describe the birth of emotions she never knew existed and how her contributions to the life of a child are reciprocated with immeasurable rewards of joy, love and fulfillment. She kept her layout simple but had fun with a multimedia title.

Kim Toomay, Olathe, Kansas

Supplies: Patterned paper (Chatterbox); textured cardstock (Bazzill); letter button (Junkitz); letter cut-outs (Foofala); metal label holder, photo turn, hinge (Making Memories); mini brads (Lasting Impressions, Making Memories); ribbon (Offray), stamping ink; vellum

A Wrong Turn

Amber took a detour on the way to her initial destination in life only to find where she ended up was where she was truly meant to be. She expresses on a printed transparency she created herself the good fortune found as a result of her unexpected series of "wrong turns" to become a wife and mother. Using a word processing program, Amber typed thesaurus variations of the word "motherly" in multiple fonts to create a subtle background and then added her journaling. Her hinged photo flips open to reveal cropped images of her treasured family.

Amber Baley, Waupun, Wisconsin

Supplies: Patterned papers (Daisy D's, Provo Craft); hinges, label holder (Making Memories); buttons (source unknown); quilt pattern (Atkinson Designs); fabric; embroidery floss; transparency; cardstock

Artist Spotlight

Shauna conducted an interview with herself to put her passion for scrapbooking in the spotlight. She created a separate journaling strip for each question, touching on her artistic strengths, inspirations and career milestones. Office elements were incorporated, such as paper clips and faux labels, and a mini folder cleverly serves as an "employee file." Tucked inside the file are reduced copies of book covers that contain her published projects. For a fun touch, Shauna replaced the "o" in her title with a framed self-portrait.

Shauna Berglund-Immel, Beaverton, Oregon
Photo: Hot Off The Press, Canby, Oregon

Supplies: Patterned paper, cardstock, tag, cardstock letter stickers, ribbons, square slide mounts, circular slide mounts, library card holders, mini file folders (Hot Off The Press); letter stamps (Hero Arts); square punch (Marvy); staples; paper clips; business card; stamping ink; pen

Monday-Friday

Although her tasks and clients often vary from day to day, Angela wanted to create a layout to show how each workday as a legal secretary has a highly regimented schedule. She printed up her typical work routine in a journaling box she created in black with white text and printed it onto white cardstock. A photo of her workspace and the incorporation of a label border bring elements of the office onto her page.

Angela Marvel, Puyallup, Washington

Supplies: Photo turns (7 Gypsies); label maker (Dymo); brads; cardstock

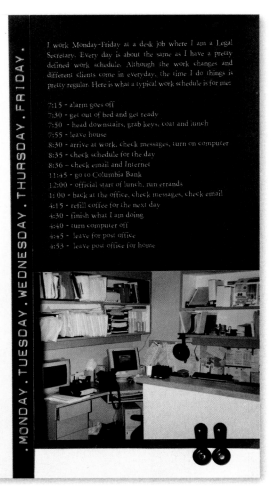

Kristin, Age 26

Staying at home to perfect a role as wife and mother was nowhere on the map. . .until Kristin was bitten by the baby bug! Her journaling-driven layout describes her unimaginable fulfillment of caring for her home and family and how she wouldn't trade her job for anything. She kept her layout simple and serene to reflect the beauty of a life she could not have planned better if she had tried.

Kristin Baxter, Valdosta, Georgia

Supplies: Patterned paper (Mara-Mi); textured cardstock (Bazzill); metal label holder (Making Memories); ribbon

A stay at home mom. How in the world did that happen?! To be honest, I never thought I would get married, much less have a child. Oh, but things changed! I met Jeff and fell in love and got married. A couple of years later, I got bit by the baby bug. Hard! Then I had my precious son. And my entire world changed. My dreams of being a career woman vanished in an instant. I now had dreams of staying home. I cannot describe how strong my desire to raise my son was. Who knew that I would wholeheartedly want to make a nice home for my husband? Well, after three years of being a "domestic goddess", I can honestly say that this is what I was meant to do. I love it! Yes, my life is pretty routine. I feel like I'm constantly cleaning and entertaining Cade. I get excited when diapers go on sale! But I also get excited when Jeff tells me how delicious dinner was. And I love the fact that my son can count on me to be there any time he needs me. So, this is certainly not where I imagined I would be at this point in my life, but now that I'm here, I wouldn't give it up for anything!

Me

When people comment about Sheila having her hands full, she smiles and knows they are very full indeed. . .of blessings. She created this page to express the many roles she plays in life, including wife, mother and artist to name just a few. Sheila printed her own border, listing many other of her accomplished titles, and used image-editing software to type descriptions for her most treasured occupations directly onto her photos

Sheila Doherty, Couer d'Alene, Idaho

Supplies: Textured cardstock (Bazzill); mini brads, metal label holder, ribbon (Making Memories); acrylic flower (KI Memories); image-editing software (Adobe Photoshop)

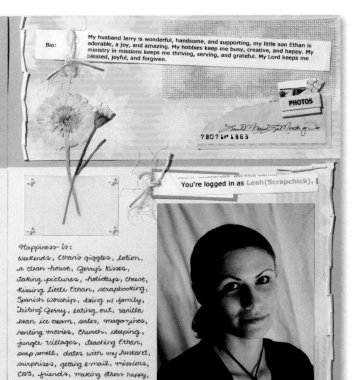

Well, I am at a point in my life right now where I feel like I've done and been through so much, yet there is still a whole lot more ahead of me, much more to come. That is very exciting. Knowing God is continually working on me and that He is fulfilling His plan for my life...wow! And I know everyday is a gift and tomorrow is not guaranteed, so I want to live each day with thankfulness, love, and ambition, and to take care in strengthening the faith I live by. For I know life on earth is just a blink of an eye compared to eternity. So right now, at age 25, it is one step of many on a never ending journey. 25 has been great, busy, exciting! I have the most precious little family all my own, we live in a wonderful house, which is my very favorite place to be, all year I've had amazing opportunities and experiences. I'm loving it! — Leah

=Current Breakdown: (as of 11/2003)=
• Happily married 5 years now
• 1st baby, Ethan, is 1½ years old
• Current missions are to Bocas del Toro in Panama
• Supporting Jerry as he is half way through internship
• Working 3 days a week in dad's office, Ethan comes too
• Scrapbook lots and now published
• Can't decide on a stable hairstyle
• Volunteer in church nursery
• Practing photography & Spanish
• Trying to manage my time more efficiently.

Happiness is:
Weekends, Ethan's giggles, lotion, a clean house, Jerry's kisses, taking pictures, holidays, cheese, kissing little Ethan, scrapbooking, Spanish worship, being w/ family, "isiting" Jerry, eating out, vanilla bean ice cream, sales, magazines, renting movies, church, sleeping, jungle villages, teaching Ethan, soap smell, dates with my husband, surprises, getting e-mail, missions, CD's, friends, making others happy, Ethan's "speach", traveling, juice, serving others, journaling, love.

Me at 25

Warmth and happiness flow from Leah's page created to examine her life at age 25. She lists her contributions to her family, her church, her God and even to herself on the left page, then reflects on what happiness means to her on the right. She also incorporated a few of her favorite things, including pressed flowers, her signature and a favorite Internet profile. Rolled edges, decorative tacks and colored mesh add texture.

Leah LaMontagne, Las Vegas, Nevada
Photos: Jerry LaMontagne, Las Vegas, Nevada

Supplies: Cardstock; letter stickers, window tag, decorative tacks, tags (Chatterbox); page pebbles, mini photos, mini negatives (Making Memories); fibers (EK Success); mesh paper (Magenta); pressed flowers, check signature; clip from Internet profile

Note to self

Think about your Gift List—not the gifts you want to buy or receive. Rather, your personal gifts. By definition, a gift is something that is bestowed voluntarily and without compensation. Likewise, talents, endowments and aptitudes are personal gifts that have been given to you with no strings attached. What are you doing with these gifts, even though nothing is necessarily expected? Do you feel a desire or obligation to share?

Consider creating a layout that showcases your personal gifts. Section your page into squares or rectangles, and list gifts from different areas of your life, such as physical, spiritual, social, mental, and the like. Ask friends and family to identify gifts they feel you possess. In addition to being emotionally rewarding, this approach will reveal personal gifts perhaps you don't know you have.

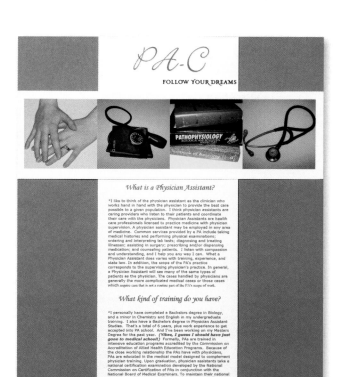

PA-C

What is a physician's assistant? Danielle developed this simple layout to answer this very question—one she gets asked at least a dozen times every day. She composed her journaling to define the role of the physician assistant as well as to describe the highlights of the profession. Danielle then documented her educational training and achievements to share the road traveled to her dreams. To achieve the graphic look of her photo arrangement, she raised the color saturation of her digital photos using image-editing software.

Danielle Layton, Clarksville, Tennessee

Supplies: Rub-on words (Making Memories); image-editing software (Hewlett Packard Photosmart software); cardstock

Crazy/Calm Life

Karen created this two-page spread to demonstrate the contrasts between the chaos of her workdays and the blissful peace of Sunday. On the left page, she randomly assembled scraps of paper and photos to capture the highlights of her crazy week and ran them off the page for a sense of perpetual motion. She printed her daily schedule to the far left and overlapped the type onto the crazy collage. The right page breathes deep with Sunday's calm, using layered strips of periwinkle papers to reflect a schedule where only church and family have a standing appointment.

Karen Huntoon, East Longmeadow, Massachusetts

Supplies: Patterned papers, cardstocks (Close To My Heart); rub-on letters, foam letter stamps (Making Memories); acrylic paints; paper scraps

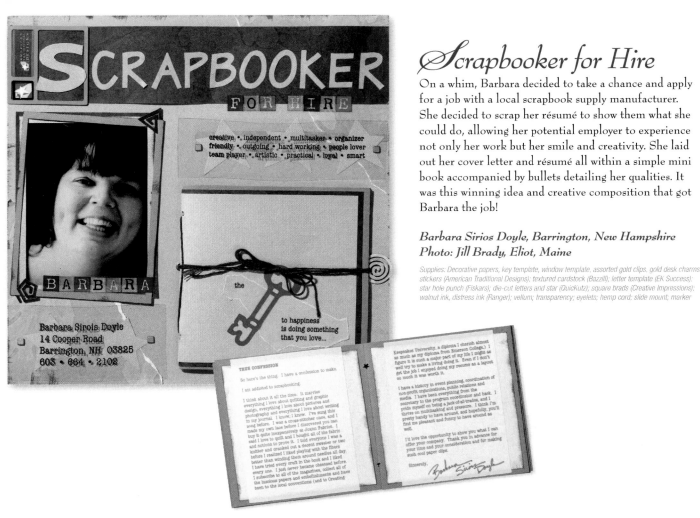

Scrapbooker for Hire

On a whim, Barbara decided to take a chance and apply for a job with a local scrapbook supply manufacturer. She decided to scrap her résumé to show them what she could do, allowing her potential employer to experience not only her work but her smile and creativity. She laid out her cover letter and résumé all within a simple mini book accompanied by bullets detailing her qualities. It was this winning idea and creative composition that got Barbara the job!

Barbara Sirios Doyle, Barrington, New Hampshire
Photo: Jill Brady, Eliot, Maine

Supplies: Decorative papers, key template, window template, assorted gold clips, gold desk charms, stickers (American Traditional Designs); textured cardstock (Bazzill); letter template (EK Success); star hole punch (Fiskars); die-cut letters and star (QuicKutz); square brads (Creative Impressions); walnut ink, distress ink (Ranger); vellum; transparency; eyelets; hemp cord; slide mount; marker

Helping Hands

Denise's hands are a huge part of her career in special education, so she designed her page to focus on her hands at work. Her journaling shares her thoughts on the power of a simple touch to let students know they are cared for and about. She attached yellow ribbon to a metal buckle with brads and adhered it to the focal photo to create the look of a handshake shared between friends. A combination of layered school-themed papers creates a sense of school-days charm.

Denise Tucker, Versailles, Indiana
Photos: Natasha Stonebraker, Aurora, Indiana

Supplies: Patterned papers (Rusty Pickle); wooden letters (Wal-Mart); metal photo turns (Jest Charming); label maker (Dymo); epoxy corner (EK Success); printed ribbon (Making Memories); metal buckle (Junkitz); distress ink (Ranger); mini brads (Artchix Studio); embossing powder; vellum

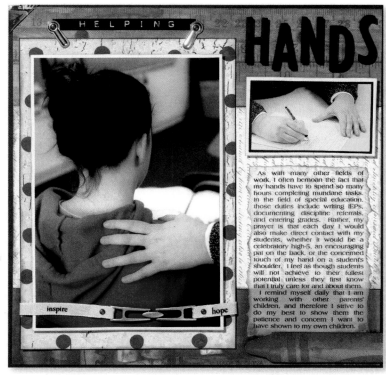

As a Young *Woman*

Just when Teri-Lynn thought she had it all figured out, her life took an unexpected turn, only to reveal unexpected blessings. She arranged and stitched her background papers to give the illusion of a quilt and evoke a homey, warm and cozy feel. Teri-Lynn carried the shine of the gold paper throughout her design by inking edges of elements with gold ink and accentuating each page with shimmering ribbons.

Teri-Lynn Masters, Truro, Nova Scotia, Canada

Supplies: Patterned papers, cut-outs (Top Line Creations); textured cardstock (Bazzill); metallic rub-ons (Craf-T); ribbon (Offray); embroidery floss; brads; eyelets; vellum; twine; stamping ink

One *Day* By the Numbers

From the numbers on the alarm clock to the number of times she tells her children to quiet down, Judith's photoless layout sums up a typical day in her life. Tags arranged in ascending order move the viewer through the figures she crunches from sunrise to sunset, including meals prepared, minutes spent pushing a stroller and number of morning snuggles. Printed twill and tape measure stickers continue the mathematical theme while floral printed letter stickers lend a feminine touch.

Judith Mara, Lancaster, Massachusetts

Supplies: Patterned papers (Mustard Moon, 7 Gypsies); textured cardstock (Bazzill); patterned cardstocks (Memories Complete); number and letter stickers (Creative Imaginations, EK Success, Memories Complete, Pebbles, Provo Craft); number stamps (PSX Design); tag template (Deluxe Designs); rub-on letters (Making Memories); printed twill (7 Gypsies); ribbons; plastic ring; staples; stamping ink; pen; brad

Mrs. *Stearns*

Colleen embraces the name she is known by to students in her cherished role as a middle-school teacher on this innovative "page." The entire tribute says "school days" through and through, from a vibrantly dressed-up ruler to a mini file folder, composition book stencil, faculty identification tag, composition book paper, binder clip and more—all creatively assembled over a patterned paper-covered clipboard.

Colleen Stearns, Natrona Heights, Pennsylvania

Supplies: Patterned papers (Rusty Pickle, 7 Gypsies); textured cardstock (Bazzill); clipboard, letter stencil (Staples); ribbons (May Arts); file folder (Rusty Pickle); sticker (EK Success); label maker (Dymo); tea dye varnish, walnut ink (Delta); ruler; paper clip; acrylic paint; pen

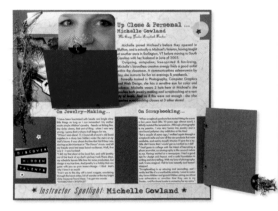

Up Close and *Personal*

The photos of Michelle in her hats inspired her "two hats" theme for this layout, which describes her two roles as a jewelry-making and scrapbooking instructor. Each hat photo lifts to share her accomplishments and dreams for each medium. The upper portion of the page shares her artist bio. Michelle added a beaded accent and shiny fibers to the page to showcase her signature obsessions.

Michelle Gowland, Bluffton, South Carolina
Photos: Maria Brown, Plattsburgh, New York

Supplies: Patterned paper (Provo Craft); hinges, star eyelets, metal letters (Making Memories); label maker (Dymo); jewelry charms (source unknown); image-editing program (Adobe Pagemaker 6.5); circle punch (Marvy); hair clip; fibers; wire; beads; cardstocks

Red

In response to the friendly teasing Nic often receives from her scrapbooking buddies about her preference for neutral, earthy tones—voilà! She created the "reddest" of red layouts just to prove she could. She even went so far as to cut out the word "red" numerous times and overlap them along the bottom for extra spunk. A chipboard frame used to spotlight her title and consequent page theme simply says it all.

Nic Howard, Pukekone, South Auckland, New Zealand

Supplies: Patterned papers (Crafter's Workshop); textured cardstocks (Bazzill); chipboard frame (Li'l Davis Designs); letter stickers (SEI); letter templates (C-Thru Ruler, Scrap Pagerz, Wordsworth); stamping ink

My scrapbooking friends have always joked with me about my unwillingness to use the colour red in my layouts. I have been teasing them that one day I will do a red layout, and what a perfect subject to scrapbook about!

Lisa At 35

Glimpses of the past, present and future pursuits of Lisa's life come together on this milestone layout. At 35, she reflects on how scrapbooking helped her transition from a career she loved in the corporate world to a career as a stay-at-home mom. To achieve the look of her artful photo, she removed the color and then re-colorized her glasses before printing the image onto pink cardstock. Whimsical patterns and accents lend an eye-catching feeling of fun.

Lisa VanderVeen, Mendham, New Jersey

Supplies: Patterned paper, patterned vellum, buttons, number stickers (American Crafts); textured cardstock (Bazzill); flower embellishments (EK Success); letter stamps (PSX Design); embroidery floss; stamping ink

Additional Instructions and Credits

Cover

Jodi created this warm and cozy page to perfectly complement Elizabeth's fun photo. She used a small file folder as a template to create larger patterned paper ones containing jotted notes of who Elizabeth is. Inked edges and foam-adhesive mounted paisley elements cut from patterned paper add visual interest.

Jodi Amidei, Memory Makers Books
Photo and page design inspiration: Elizabeth Cuzzacrea, Lockport, New York

Supplies: Patterned paper (Daisy D's, Making Memories); ribbon, staples (Making Memories); stamps, file folder template (Rusty Pickle); file label (Avery); stamping ink

P. 1 Bookplate: Me, Myself, and I

Torrey created an attractive journal comprised of patterned papers, tags and ribbons so inviting it simply begs to be written in. She covered a store-bought journal with papers, concealed the seams with ribbon and embellished the cover for a warm and personalized look.

Torrey Scott, Thornton, Colorado

Supplies: Patterned paper (Daisy D's); acrylic letters (Li'l Davis Designs); cardstock; ribbon

P. 6 Editor

Here Emily carries her role of book editor into her page design. Text-patterned papers, file folders, folio closures and a library pocket displaying proofreaders' symbols capture the essence of her word-driven vocation in a creative way.

Emily Curry Hitchingham, Memory Makers Books
Photo: Ken Trujillo

Supplies: Patterned papers (7 Gypsies, Autumn Leaves); file folders, library card and pocket (Autumn Leaves); punches (EK Success, Family Treasures, Nankong); clip (Design Originals); metal flowers (Nunn Design); folio closures (Colorbök); stickers (Destination Scrapbook Designs)

P. 8 Favorites Tag Book
Alecia Ackerman Grimm, Atlanta, Georgia

Supplies: Patterned paper (Colorbök, KI Memories); textured cardstocks (Bazzill); paper flower (Prima); quote (KI Memories); letter stickers (Creative Imaginations, Karen Foster Design, KI Memories, SEI); foam letter stamps, ribbon, blue staples (Making Memories); crystal lacquer (Sakura Hobby Craft); metal tag (Chronicle Books); distress ink (Ranger); mini file folders (handmade); button (Junkitz); vellum flowers (EK Success), flower-picking image (downloaded from internet); fibers (Great Balls Of Fiber); silk flower (Wal-Mart); charm (source unknown); party tile (Target); foam stamp (Plaid); tag (DMD); rub-on letters (source unknown); letter stamp (Stamp Craft); charm (source unknown); striped fabric; trim and fabric strips; rhinestones; acrylic paint; stamping ink; staples; pen; large binder ring

P. 8 Tidbits About Me
Melissa Godin, Lorne, New Brunswick, Canada

Supplies: Patterned papers, page tabs (KI Memories); letter stamps (Ma Vinci's Reliquary); assorted stamps (PSX Design); letter stickers (Chatterbox); definition stickers (Making Memories); twist tie (Pebbles); metal-rimmed tags, brads, rub-ons, ribbons (Making Memories); photo corners (Canson); staples; ribbon; silk flowers; stamping ink

P. 9 Colleen
Colleen Stearns, Natrona Heights, Pennsylvania

Supplies: Patterned papers (Paper Adventures, Rusty Pickle); belt loop (7 Gypsies); ribbon, color wash spray (Scrapping With Style); small, medium and large tags (Rusty Pickle); paper flowers, rub-ons (Making Memories); metal word tag (Happy Hammer); label maker (Dymo); heart charm (source unknown); brown paper lunch bags; buttons; staples; lace; silk flowers; safety pins; walnut ink

P. 10 Thankful Box and Blessing Booklet
Cheryl Mezzetti, Weymouth, Massachusetts

Thankful Box Supplies: Patterned papers (K & Company, Karen Foster Design, Provo Craft, Scenic Route Paper Co., Scrap Ease); ribbons (May Arts); rub-ons (Making Memories); hinge (Sticker Studio); watermark pen (Tsukineko); acrylic paints; clear embossing powder; silk flowers; letter stencil; brads

Blessing Book Supplies: Patterned papers (K & Company, Karen Foster Design, Provo Craft, Scenic Route Paper Co., Scrap Ease); wooden frame (Li'l Davis Designs); cardstock (Bazzill); canvas (Daisy D's); tags (Avery, Pebbles); label maker (Dymo); ribbons (May Arts); letter stencil (Autumn Leaves); metal paper clip, destination washer, safety pins, brads, photo turns (Making Memories); word tags (Pebbles); letter cut-outs (Foofala); library pocket; round hole punch; color wash; stamping ink

P. 11 Finding Me Again
Colleen Stearns, Natrona Heights, Pennsylvania

Supplies: Patterned papers, card keeper, tags, chipboard letters (Rusty Pickle); paper flowers (Prima); distress ink (Ranger); pen; lace, silk flower; ribbon

P. 12 Did You Know This About Me?

Fun facts about Suzy are revealed on inked strips of paper with a different font for each insight. Suzy designed her page with multiple patterns and soft, feminine colors that complement her photo and capture her happy persona. In addition to her journaling strips, Suzy included a journaling box that celebrates the primary source of her joy—her family.

Suzy West, Fremont, California

Supplies: Patterned papers, square tacks (Chatterbox); pewter charm (Making Memories); metal clips (Limited Edition Rubberstamps); letter stickers (EK Success); label maker (Dymo); silk flower; stamping ink

P. 24 My Thoughts on Aging

Crinkly, bumpy textures may fill Shannon's page on aging, but her photos reveal a timeless, carefree spirit. She crumpled number tissue paper and adhered it to textured paper for effect and hid her journaling beneath the flip-up paper block beneath her title. Shannon created her page with the conclusion that she will always remain a young 20-something in her mind. Brown tones and gold accents lend an autumn feeling to the layout, with glints of shimmer and shine to add a playful attitude, much like Shannon's.

Shannon Taylor, Bristol, Tennessee
Photos: Robert Taylor, Bristol Tennessee

Supplies: Textured papers (Artistic Scrapper, Magic Scraps); number tissue paper, walnut ink (7 Gypsies); metal label holder, date charm, eyelet (Making Memories); nailheads (Magic Scraps); rubber strip, circle metal finding (Anima Designs); cheesecloth (Wal-Mart); title letter brads (Provo Craft); gold leafing pen (Krylon); liquid gesso (Golden Artist Colors); brads

P. 36 Believe

A reflection on her faith is at the heart of Sheila's layout as she describes her thoughts on the difference between religion and her personal relationship with Jesus. While the left side evokes a solemn, prayerful quality, the bulk of the page is filled with jewel-tone colors and carefully constructed journaling with highlighted headlines. She carried the circular pattern of her paper across the page using a corner rounder on the journaling block and a circle cutter and punch to create the printed curve and Scripture accent.

Sheila Doherty, Coeur d'Alene, Idaho

Supplies: Patterned papers (Crossed Paths); corner rounder (Carl); circle punch (Marvy); circle cutter (Provo Craft); ribbons (Michaels); cardstock; stamping ink

P. 48 This I Know

The one thing that Stacey is certain of is that uncertainty has filled her life with more happiness than she could have ever imagined. She designed this open and honest page with a laid-back feel through grungy patterned papers and cork title letters. She had her husband shoot this photo specifically for this page, to share what life has taught her so far—especially how the best things in life are quite often unexpected.

Stacey Wakelin, Surrey, British Columbia, Canada
Photo: Scott Wakelin, Surrey, British Columbia, Canada

Supplies: Patterned papers (Basic Grey, Karen Foster Design); photo corners (Canson); cork paper (Magic Scraps); letter stamps (PSX Design); brads, rub-on words (Making Memories); eyelet brads (Pebbles); elastic cording (Darice); cardstocks; stamping ink

P. 60 In My Life

The instant a child enters your life, previous goals and ambitions can quickly change, as Julie describes in her layout. Heart-warming colors, homey patterns and soft rounded edges carry on the serene feel of her photo, and a pullout tag tucked inside the embellished library pocket reveals the beaming face of her son—a reminder of all Julie has gained in place of the material rewards put on hold.

Julie Johnson, Seabrook, Texas
Photo: Angie Head for Family Memories, Friendswood, Texas

Supplies: Textured cardstock (Prism Papers); patterned paper (Daisy D's); decorative brads (Making Memories); ribbon buckles (Nunn Design); chalk ink (Clearsnap); metal decorative accent (source unknown); ribbon; silk flowers

P. 72 The Quest

The real, true and "x-traordinary" moments of Shelley's family became the driving force behind her desire to dive deep into photography. Her layout displays several of those treasured moments now preserved along with an image of herself armed with her camera. This page expresses her heart and purpose behind the camera lens and her hopes that those captured moments will live on.

Shelley Rankin, Fredericton, New Brunswick, Canada

Supplies: Patterned papers (Chatterbox, Mustard Moon, Paper Loft); word stencils (Autumn Leaves); letter stencils (Making Memories); printed circle, square conchos (Scrapworks); chipboard letters (Chatterbox); dimensional adhesive (JudiKins); stamping ink

P. 84 Home Birth

People always ask Jessie why she wanted to have a home birth. This layout was created to express the reasons behind her choice and to capture the beauty of this most joyous event. To give the page a dreamy effect, Jessie used filters in her image-editing software to soften the image of her photograph and continued the look by distressing the title with paint. Her poetic journaling shares what she did and did not want her birth experience to be like and celebrates her miraculous achievement.

Jessie Baldwin, Las Vegas, Nevada

Supplies: Textured cardstock (Bazzill); letter stickers (Deluxe Designs); rub-on letters (Heidi Swapp); date stamp (Making Memories); printed transparency strip (Autumn Leaves); stamping ink; acrylic paint

P. 96 It All Adds Up

When Jenn began calculating the numbers of diaper changes, months pregnant, doctor visits and other totals involved with raising four boys, she had to create a page to document the astronomical figures! She created the photo mat for the focal photo by placing letter stencils over artist scratchboard and scratching the word "Love." The exhaustive details are endearingly offset with happy images and whimsical details.

Jenn Brookover, San Antonio, Texas

Supplies: Patterned paper (Carolee's Creations, Sweetwater); printed twill (7 Gypsies); ribbon, metal number (Making Memories); buttons (Blumenthal Lansing); letter stickers (Creative Imaginations); artist scratchboard (Ampersand Art Supply); solvent ink (Tsukineko); letter stencils (source unknown); stamping ink; acrylic paint; chalk; floss

Resources

Book:

Klauser, Henriette. *Write It Down, Make It Happen: Knowing What You Want and Getting It.* New York: Touchstone, 2001

Web sites:

www.dictionary.com
www.ethicalwill.com

Source Guide

The following companies manufacture products featured in this book. Please check your local retailers to find these materials, or go to a company's Web site for the latest product. In addition, we have made every attempt to properly credit the items mentioned in this book. We apologize to any company that we have listed incorrectly, and we would appreciate hearing from you.

3M
(800) 364-3577
www.3m.com

7 Gypsies
(800) 588-6707
www.7gypsies.com

A.C. Moore
www.acmoore.com

Accu-Cut®
(800) 288-1670
www.accucut.com

Adobe Systems Incorporated
(866) 766-2256
www.adobe.com

All My Memories
(888) 553-1998
www.allmymemories.com

All Night Media
(see Plaid Enterprises)

American Art Clay Co. (AMACO)
(800) 374-1600
www.amaco.com

American Crafts
(801) 226-0747
www.americancrafts.com

American Tag Company
(800) 223-3956
www.americantag.net

American Traditional Designs®
(800) 448-6656
www.americantraditional.com

Ampersand Art Supply
(800) 822-1939
www.ampersandart.com

Amscan, Inc.
(800) 444-8887
www.amscan.com

Anima Designs
(800) 570-6847
www.animadesigns.com

Anna Griffin, Inc.
(888) 817-8170
www.annagriffin.com

ARTchix Studio
(250) 370-9985
www.artchixstudio.com

Artistic Scrapper
(818) 786-8304
www.artisticscrapper.com

Atkinson Designs, Inc.
(763) 441-1825
www.atkinsondesigns.com

Autumn Leaves
(800) 588-6707
www.autumnleaves.com

Avery Dennison Corporation
(800) GO-AVERY
www.avery.com

Basic Grey™
(801) 451-6006
www.basicgrey.com

Bazzill Basics Paper
(480) 558-8557
www.bazzillbasics.com

Beads & Plenty More
(517) 47-BEADS
www.beadsandplentymore.com

Blumenthal Lansing Company
(201) 935-6220
www.buttonsplus.com

Bobbin Ribbon - no contact info

Bo-Bunny Press
(801) 771-4010
www.bobunny.com

Boutique Trims, Inc.
(248) 437-2017
www.boutiquetrims.com

Boxer Scrapbook Productions
(503) 625-0455
www.boxerscrapbooks.com

BraidCraft - no contact info

Bunch Of Fun- no contact info

Canson®, Inc.
(800) 628-9283
www.canson-us.com

Card Connection- see Michaels

CARL Mfg. USA, Inc.
(800) 257-4771
www.Carl-Products.com

Carolee's Creations®
(435) 563-1100
www.ccpaper.com

Carole Fabrics, Inc.
(706) 863-4742
www.carolefabrics.com

Charming Place, A
(509) 325-5655
www.acharmingplace.com

Chatterbox, Inc.
(208) 939-9133
www.chatterboxinc.com

Chronicle Books
(800) 722-6656
www.chroniclebooks.com

Clearsnap, Inc.
(360) 293-6634
www.clearsnap.com

Close To My Heart®
(888) 655-6552
www.closetomyheart.com

Club Scrap™, Inc.
(888) 634-9100
www.clubscrap.com

Colorbök™, Inc.
(800) 366-4660
www.colorbok.com

Colors by Design
(800) 832-8436
www.colorsbydesign.com

Cost Plus World Market
(510) 893-7300
www.costplus.com

Crafter's Workshop, The
(877) CRAFTER
www.thecraftersworkshop.com

Craf-T Products
(507) 235-3996
www.craf-tproducts.com

Crafts, Etc. Ltd.
(800) 888-0321
www.craftsetc.com

Creative Imaginations
(800) 942-6487
www.cigift.com

Creative Impressions Rubber Stamps, Inc.
(719) 596-4860
www.creativeimpressions.com

Creative Memories®
(800) 468-9335
www.creativememories.com

Creek Bank Creations, Inc.
(217) 427-5980
www.creekbankcreations.com

Crossed Paths™
(972) 393-3755
www.crossedpaths.net

Cross-My Heart-Cards, Inc.
(888) 689-8808
www.crossmyheart.com

C-Thru® Ruler Company, The
(Wholesale only)
(800) 243-8419
www.cthruruler.com

Daisy D's Paper Company
(888) 601-8955
www.daisydspaper.com

Daisy Hill - no contact info

Darice, Inc.
(800) 321-1494
www.darice.com

Delta Technical Coatings, Inc.
(800) 423-4135
www.deltacrafts.com

Deluxe Designs
(480) 497-9005
www.deluxedesigns.com

Design Originals
(800) 877-0067
www.d-originals.com

Designs by Reminisce
(319) 358-9777
www.shopreminisce.com

Destination™ Scrapbook Designs
(866) 806-7826
www.destinationstickers.com

DieCuts with a View™
(877) 221-6107
www.dcwv.com

DMD Industries, Inc.
(800) 805-9890
www.dmdind.com

Doodlebug Design™ Inc.
(801) 966-9952
www.doodlebug.ws

Dymo
www.dymo.com

EK Success™, Ltd.
(800) 524-1349
www.eksuccess.com

Emagination Crafts, Inc.
(866) 238-9770
www.emaginationcrafts.com

Family Treasures, Inc.®
www.familytreasures.com

Fiber Scraps™
(215) 230-4905
www.fiberscraps.com

Fiskars®, Inc.
(800) 950-0203
www.fiskars.com

Flair® Designs
(888) 546-9990
www.flairdesignsinc.com

FLAX art & design
(415) 552-2355
www.flaxart.com

FontWerks
(604) 942-3105
www.fontwerks.com

FoofaLa
(402) 330-3208
www.foofala.com

Frances Meyer, Inc.®
(413) 584-5446
www.francesmeyer.com

Frazzles - no contact info

Funky Fibers - no contact info

Gartner Studios, Inc.
www.uprint.com

Gary M. Burlin & Co.
(800) 659-PENS
www.garymburlin.com

Golden Artist Colors, Inc.
(800) 959-6543
www.goldenpaints.com

Go West Studios
(214) 227-0007
www.goweststudios.com

Grafix®
(800) 447-2349
www.grafix.com

Graphic Products Corporation
(800) 323-1658
www.gpcpapers.com

Great Balls of Fiber
(303) 697-5942
www.greatballsoffiber.com

Hampton Art Stamps, Inc.
(800) 229-1019
www.hamptonart.com

Happy Hammer, The
(303) 690-3883
www.thehappyhammer.com

Heidi Grace Designs
(866) 89heidi
www.heidigrace.com

Heidi Swapp/Advantus Corporation
(904) 482-0092
www.heidiswapp.com

Hero Arts® Rubber Stamps, Inc.
(800) 822-4376
www.heroarts.com

Hewlett-Packard Company
www.hp.com/go/scrapbooking

Hobby Lobby Stores, Inc.
www.hobbylobby.com

Home Depot U.S.A., Inc.
www.homedepot.com

Hot Off The Press, Inc.
(800) 227-9595
www.paperpizazz.com

Hunt Corporation
(800) 879-4868
www.hunt-corp.com

Imagination Project, Inc.
(513) 860-2711
www.imaginationproject.com

Inkadinkado® Rubber Stamps
(800) 888-4652
www.inkadinkado.com

Jaquard Products/Rupert, Gibbon & Spider, Inc.
(800) 442-0455
www.jacquardproducts.com

Jest Charming
(702) 564-5101
www.jestcharming.com

JewelCraft, LLC
(201) 223-0804
www.jewelcraft.biz

Jo-Ann Stores
(888) 739-4120
www.joann.com

JudiKins
(310) 515-1115
www.judikins.com

Junkitz™
(732) 792-1108
www.junkitz.com

K & Company
(888) 244-2083
www.kandcompany.com

Karen Foster Design
(801) 451-9779
www.karenfosterdesign.com

Keeping Memories Alive™
(800) 419-4949
www.scrapbooks.com

KI Memories
(972) 243-5595
www.kimemories.com

Krylon®
(216) 566-200
www.krylon.com

La Pluma, Inc.
(803) 749-4076
www.debrabeagle.com

Lasting Impressions for Paper, Inc.
(801) 298-1979
www.lastingimpressions.com

Leather Factory, The
(800) 433-3201
www.leatherfactory.com

Leave Memories
www.leavememories.com

Li'l Davis Designs
(949) 838-0344
www.lildavisdesigns.com

Limited Edition Rubberstamps
(650) 594-4242
www.limitededitionrs.com

Lincraft
www.lincraft.com.au

Lion Brand Yarn Company
www.lionbrand.com

Little Black Dress Designs
(360) 894-8844
www.littleblackdressdesigns.com

Magenta Rubber Stamps
(800) 565-5254
www.magentastyle.com

Magic Mesh
(651) 345-6374
www.magicmesh.com

Magic Scraps™
(972) 238-1838
www.magicscraps.com

Magnetic Poetry®
(800) 370-7697
www.magneticpoetry.com

Making Memories
(800) 286-5263
www.makingmemories.com

Manto Fev™
(402) 505-3752
www.mantofev.com

Mara-Mi, Inc.
(800) 627-2648
www.mara-mi.com

Marvy® Uchida/ Uchida of America, Corp.
(800) 541-5877
www.uchida.com

Ma Vinci's Reliquary
http://crafts.dm.net/
mall/reliquary/

May Arts
(800) 442-3950
www.mayarts.com

me & my BiG ideas®
(949) 883-2065
www.meandmybigideas.com

Memories Complete™, LLC
(866) 966-6365
www.memoriescomplete.com

Memories in the Making/Leisure Arts
(800) 643-8030
www.leisurearts.com

Meri Meri
www.merimeri.com

Michaels® Arts & Crafts
(800) 642-4235
www.michaels.com

Mill Hill
www.millhillbeads.com

MoBe' Stamps!
(925) 443-2101
www.mobestamps.com

Mrs. Grossman's Paper Company
(800) 429-4549
www.mrsgrossmans.com

Mustard Moon™
(408) 299-8542
www.mustardmoon.com

My Imaginary Room - no contact info

Mystic Press
(480) 242-2698
www.mysticpress.com

Nankong Enterprises, Inc.
(302) 731-2995
www.nankong.com

Neenah Paper, inc.
(678) 566-6500
www.neenah.com

Nunn Design
(360) 379-3557
www.nunndesign.com

Office Depot
www.officedepot.com

Offray
www.offray.com

On The Surface
(847) 675-2520

Paper Adventures®
(800) 525-3196
www.paperadventures.com

Paper Company, The/ANW Crestwood
(800) 525-3196
www.anwcrestwood.com

Paper Fever, Inc.
(800) 477-0902
www.paperfever.com

Paper Loft
(866) 254-1961
www.paperloft.com

Paper Studio - no contact info

Patchwork Paper Design, Inc.
(239) 481-4823
www.patchworkpaper.com

Pebbles Inc.
(801) 224-1857
www.pebblesinc.com

Pioneer Photo Albums, Inc.®
(800) 366-3686
www.pioneerphotoalbums.com

Plaid Enterprises, Inc.
(800) 842-4197
www.plaidonline.com

PM Designs
(888) 595-2887
www.designsbypm.com

Polyform Products Co.
(847) 427-0020
www.sculpey.com

Postmodern Design
(405) 321-3176
www.stampdiva.com

Prima
(909) 627-5532
www.mulberrypaperflowers.com

Prism® Papers
(866) 902-1002
www.prismpapers.com

Provo Craft®
(888) 577-3545
www.provocraft.com

PSX Design™
(800) 782-6748
www.psxdesign.com

Punch Bunch, The
(254) 791-4209
www.thepunchbunch.com

QuicKutz
(801) 765-1144
www.quickutz.com

Raindrops on Roses
(307) 877-6241
www.raindropsonroses.com

Ranger Industries, Inc.
(800) 244-2211
www.rangerink.com

Rusty Pickle
(801) 746-1045
www.rustypickle.com

Sakura Hobby Craft
(310) 212-7878
www.sakuracraft.com

Scenic Route Paper Co.
(801) 785-0761
www.scenicroutepaper.com

Scrap Ease®
(800) 272-3874
www.whatsnewltd.com

Scrap Pagerz™
(435) 645-0696
www.scrappagerz.com

Scrappin' Extras™/Punch Crazy Scrapbooking
(403) 271-9649
www.scrappinextras.com

Scrapping With Style
(704) 254-6238
www.scrappingwithstyle.com

Scrapworks, LLC
(801) 363-1010
www.scrapworks.com

SEI, Inc.
(800) 333-3279
www.shopsei.com

Sizzix®
(866) 742-4447
www.sizzix.com

Spellbinders™ Paper Arts, LLC
(888) 547-0400
www.spellbinders.us

Stamp Craft - see Plaid Enterprises

Stampers Anonymous/The Creative Block
(888) 326-0012
www.stampersanonymous.com

Stampin' Up!®
(800) 782-6787
www.stampinup.com

Stamp It! - no contact info

Staples, Inc.
(800) 3STAPLE
www.staples.com

Sticker Studio™
(208) 322-2465
www.stickerstudio.com

Strathmore Papers
(800) 628-8816
www.strathmore.com

Sulyn Industries, Inc.
(800) 257-8596
www.sulyn.com

Suze Weinberg Design Studio
(732) 761-2400
www.schmoozewithsuze.com

Sweetwater
(800) 359-3094
www.sweetwaterscrapbook.com

Target
www.target.com

Timeless Touches™/Dove Valley Productions, LLC
(623) 362-8285
www.timelesstouches.net

Top Line Creations™
(866) 954-0559
www.topline-creations.com

Trims and Buttons, Inc.
(213) 689-9110
www.buttons4u.com

Triplets- no contact info

Tsukineko®, Inc.
(800) 769-6633
www.tsukineko.com

U.S. Stamp & Sign Co.- no contact info

Wal-Mart Stores, Inc.
(800) WALMART
www.walmart.com

Walnut Hollow® Farm, Inc.
(800) 950-5101
www.walnuthollow.com

Wendy Bellisimo- no contact info

Westrim® Crafts
(800) 727-2727
www.westrimcrafts.com

Wordsworth
(719) 282-3495
www.wordsworthstamps.com

Wrights® Ribbon Accents
(877) 597-4448
www.wrights.com

Xyron
(800) 793-3523
www.xyron.com

Index